THE
JESUS
MEDITATIONS

THE JESUS MEDITATIONS

A GUIDE FOR CONTEMPLATION

MICHAEL KENNEDY, S.J.

With accompanying CD narrated by
MARTIN SHEEN

A Crossroad Book
The Crossroad Publishing Company
New York

The Crossroad Publishing Company
481 Eighth Avenue, New York, NY 10001

Scripture citations are taken from *Christian Community Bible: Catholic Pastoral Edition*, 14th ed., copyright © 1994 by Bernardo Huralt, used with permission of Claretian Publications, U.P. P.O. Box 4, Quezon City 1101, Philippines.

Printed in the United States of America

Library of Congress Cataloging-in-Publication Data

Kennedy, Michael.
  The Jesus meditations : a guide for contemplation / by Michael Kennedy ;
  with accompanying CD narrated by Martin Sheen.
      p.   cm.
    ISBN 0-8245-1929-9
    1. Jesus Christ – Meditations. 2. Bible. N.T. Gospels – Meditations.
  3. Catholic Church – Prayer-books and devotions – English.   I. Title.
  BT306.43 .k46 2002
  232 – dc21

                                                                  2001005986

1   2   3   4   5   6   7   8   9   10   08   07   06   05   04   03   02

To Luis Olivares, C.F.M.,
Meliss Wade,
Ruth and Eugene Kennedy.
You have inspired me and made me who I am.
May you rest in peace.

contents

preface

Over the years, numerous people who use these meditations have suggested making recordings, for use in both their own personal prayer and with groups. Two key contributors to the project were Janne Shirley, a chaplain at Central Juvenile Hall in Los Angeles, and Arturo Lopez, the director of the Guadalupano Homeless Project at Dolores Mission Church. Janne has led meditations for years and reads the gospel passages on the CD. Arturo has accompanied most of the meditations on guitar at Dolores Mission. His natural, graceful playing provides the background to these meditations on the CD.

Our obvious choice to read the meditations was Martin Sheen because of his wonderful voice, his familiarity with the meditations, his personal friendship with the Dolores Mission community, and his own commitment to and love for Jesus. When I asked Martin, he generously and enthusiastically said yes. He asked me to give him the meditations right away because he wanted to get the feel of them. When you listen to the meditations selected from this book you will be brought into a gospel scene, into an encounter with Jesus and other people from the Gospels. Martin's goal was to get inside the person of Jesus and be able communicate this feeling in the recording.

I still remember Martin reading a meditation on healing with a good friend of ours, Fr. Luis Olivares, C.F.M., who was dying at Cedars-Sinai Hospital. Through his reading, Martin conveyed the deep wave of compassion we all shared around the hospital bed. More recently, Martin read a meditation on the suffering of Jesus during a Good Friday service at Central Juvenile Hall. There was something magical about the way he was able to put himself into the meditation. We had a strong sense of the One who went before us identifying with these incarcerated young men and women, listening to how Jesus suffered as they do.

I invite you to listen to these meditations, in the hope that they lead you into a deep, prayerful experience of Jesus. You can follow the written text, or simply experience the meditations by listening to the CD. I suggest finding a place where you won't be disturbed and where you can relax and allow the meditations to engage your imagination. You should feel free to listen to the meditations several times, become familiar with them, and return to what moves you in prayer.

acknowledgments

I treasure the people with whom I work in Los Angeles. The adventure of putting this book together has not been a solitary one. Actually, it would have been impossible without a wonderful, supportive community.

I am deeply grateful to those people who were willing to share their personal stories, which are of central importance to this book: Greg Boyle, S.J., Mary Ellen Burton-Christie, Laura Clark, Mario Fuentes, Oscar Galindo, Bill Garcia, Cassandra Gonzalez, Dick Howard, Martha Lujan, Frank Montejano, Tanya Quille, M.D., Mark Raper, S.J., Marlon Rivera, Rob Smith, Juan Vargas, Bishop Gabino Zavala.

Bernardo Gantier, S.J., an artist from Bolivia, used the meditations found in this book for a year in his personal daily prayer, from which he drew the inspiration to create the beautiful drawings found in this book.

Martin Sheen, as always, was gracious and accommodating. He took two of his Sundays to record the meditations found on the CD that accompanies this book. Janne Shirley and Arturo Lopez also contributed to the production of the CD. They are important people in my life, and I am glad they could participate in the creation of the CD.

Richard Kaplan of Indigo Ranch Studio in Malibu, California, and Charlton Pettus of Sherman Oaks, California, gave their time, expertise, and great talent to the recording, mixing, and every other technical aspect of the CD. Without them, it could never have happened.

Mary Ellen and Doug Burton-Christie, Eddy Martinez, Mike Roide, and Michael Engh, S.J. have helped with many of the details of this book. These are great traveling companions with wonderful insights, great questions, and encouraging words.

John Lipson, whose long hours organizing, arranging, and helping made this book possible.

I have so much enjoyed working again with The Crossroad Publishing Company, especially Paul McMahon and Gwendolin Herder. It is a pleasure and grace to work with them.

Lastly, I would like to thank my Jesuit community in East Los Angeles: Bill Ameche, Greg Boyle, Bill Cain, Robert Dolan, Mike Engh, Ted Gabrielli, Elias Puentes, and Mark Torres.

I am grateful for this community of friends. Life and this book would have a different color — and less beauty — without them.

introduction

On a warm March afternoon, I walked along the dark corridor of Twin Towers jail in downtown Los Angeles. I was on my way to visit Krystal, a seventeen-year-old African-American girl who had recently been sentenced to thirteen years in state prison.

Krystal was in isolation, or "the hole," because she was a minor and was not allowed to be housed on the general population floors above. When I reached the cell, Krystal smiled broadly and we sat down together.

We talked for a long time. At one point she said, "Fr. Mike, I am so glad I met you. You helped me to be closer to God. I have learned how to use my imagination in meeting Jesus in the Bible. I have not been outside of this darkness or felt the sun on my face for a month. I have survived being in the hole because of my faith life. By using the meditations, I have felt the touch of Jesus. After being in this hole and reflecting on my life, I know that I learned a lot during the Wednesday meditation sessions and the all-day retreats while I was in Central Juvenile Hall. Thanks."

As I left this dark, windowless building, I reflected on how grateful I was for the retreat experience and for times of meditation with Krystal and many others during the previous months. God had been really present at those times, especially during the retreats. I recalled how, after a retreat, a young man named James said to me, "Fr. Mike, I really never have been into God, but what happened at the retreat was so strong that I really felt that God was right there. It was like I was being touched by a powerful Presence. I still feel this. When is the next retreat?"

A few months after my visit with Krystal, I celebrated the feast of St. Ignatius on July 31 at Dolores Mission Church, our parish in East

Los Angeles. Elias, a twenty-eight-year-old young man who soon would be entering the Society of Jesus, stood up and said, "Two years ago I had hardly heard of St. Ignatius. All I knew was he had founded a religious order. As I now stand before you, I have lived with eight Jesuits for a year. I have seen how St. Ignatius's vision and his method of meditating on the Gospels affects everything they do. I've also learned the method, and the meditations have changed my life too. St. Ignatius may have lived hundreds of years ago, but his spirit, his dream of finding God in all things, and especially among the most needy, is still alive in those who follow him. My job here in the parish has been to care for fifty homeless men who sleep in this church every night. The vision of Ignatius has deepened my commitment to the poor, which has changed my life." As I looked at the faces in the congregation, felt the stillness in the church, and saw the flowing of tears, I knew that they had been moved by Elias's simple testimony of faith.

After Elias finished speaking, I asked the congregation what it meant for them to belong to a parish with others who follow the dream of St. Ignatius. Rita stood up and said, "For three years, we have been learning how to meditate. I know this way of prayer originates from St. Ignatius, who believed in connecting to God with the heart as well as using the imagination with a gospel story to know Jesus better. I know he wrote a small book called the *Spiritual Exercises* in which he explains how to use our imagination in prayer. This method has brought us closer to Jesus and given us strength in our darkest moments." Then she began to cry.

I flashed back a few months. I remembered standing with Rita near her brother, who had just been killed in a drive-by shooting. He was her second brother to have been killed. I recalled being with Rita, her mother, and her family in that cold, damp room in the huge monster of County Hospital in Los Angeles. Rita brought her family through that tragic moment. The presence of Jesus in her life, through the meditations she did in the small faith communities of the parish, gave her the inner strength to support her family, devastated by such a senseless killing. She finished her sharing that evening in the church by saying, "I am so grateful for being in a parish that is so committed to prayer and to justice."

Listening to Krystal, Elias, and Rita reminded me why I have chosen to put more emphasis on meditation in groups rather than just on Bible study. Meditation helps people to truly experience God in their lives.

It is clear how these people have experienced Jesus through their faith lives, in community, and through their practice of meditation. When Elias and Rita shared concrete examples of this at the service for St. Ignatius, they manifested how they have been transformed. An important aspect of their transformation was the connection made in their lives between the journey within and the journey without. Knowing Jesus through meditation with the community is personally transformative. Embracing his values results in concrete change in daily life. The meditation practice that Krystal, Rita, and Elias learned changed them from within. It gave them a vision so that their life choices are now distinct from those of others. It is no accident that Rita adopted her brother's three children, faces the problem of violence by working for a safer community, travels to the state capitol as an advocate for human rights for immigrants, and feeds the homeless with the small faith community to which she belongs. The goal of gospel meditation is to transform us within so that we can help transform our world.

Jesus was clear that we will be judged by what we do with our lives. Did we love unconditionally? Did we house the homeless, visit the sick, the prisoners? I hope that the inner transformation that comes through meditation, either individually or in groups, will spill over into the decisions and actions of daily life. This method of meditation is not an escape from reality but rather a deepening of a vision of the One who gave his life for others. In this encounter we are moved to act.

Jesus envisioned a world in which we can all live as brothers and sisters. Jesus attempted to live out the dream that he received from his Abba. He was willing to face the consequences of living out that dream. Jesus and his dream captured the heart of Ignatius.

After celebrating the feast day of Ignatius in our parish church, Elias and I walked along a darkened street by our house in East Los Angeles. The fog had settled in for the night. During our walk I could not help but feel a little of what the disciples felt on their way to Emmaus as they listened to a stranger — Jesus. Their hearts were aflame. To try to follow

Jesus as Ignatius and so many others who have passionately desired something better for this world have done, does set your heart on fire. Spending time in meditation opens our hearts so that the passion and dream of Jesus can be kindled within. As I walked that July night with Elias past newly painted graffiti on the walls, I realized once again we don't have to walk alone in this life. In fact, it is too difficult to maintain the dream of Jesus without the support of others to walk with us. How important it is to have companions on the way. This is true of meditation as well. After you have experienced meditation, I suggest you share it with others. Something more happens in the moment of sharing. As we share our story with fellow travelers on the journey, our hearts can burn like the hearts of the disciples walking to Emmaus.

Krystal and her best friend, Nancy, are truly traveling companions. They were in Central Juvenile Hall for almost a year together. Nancy had lost her baby and, because she was locked up, she was not able to attend the funeral. For many months we talked about having a service to bring closure around the death of her baby. As we planned the service, we decided to use the meditation "Healed," which is found in this book.

To remember Nancy's baby and to acknowledge her loss, ten of us gathered in a circle in a dimly lit chapel. One of those present was Javier, the chaplain at Juvenile Hall. I asked everyone to recall one person, someone to whom they were close, who had died recently. I asked them to remember the last time they saw this person alive. Nancy then told the story of her son's death. We each asked for the grace of healing. Javier read the Gospel. We put on some quiet music and I slowly read the meditation.

After the meditation, Nancy took oil and anointed each of our hands with a prayer for healing. We felt profound depth and stillness in that chapel, and we all were moved to tears. We each wrote a letter to our loved one who had died. Javier shared that he and his wife, Irma, had lost their baby, and that he had not been able to grieve until that evening. He was deeply touched and felt very connected to Nancy, who had also lost her baby. While holding a burning candle, one person shared something about his or her experience of loss. Then the candle was passed to another, who shared his or her story. The candle gently illuminated each tear-streaked face. The service ended with Nancy sharing a prayer for her baby.

We can use the same method of meditation in our parish small base communities, in hospitals, in jails, in universities or high schools. It can always be adapted to the needs of particular groups. After using this method with widely varied groups over a long period of time, I have found a consistent dynamic as people practice the meditation. As they become familiar with the method, they become free to concentrate on the content of the meditation and their own inner movements rather than focusing on what might be coming next.

For those who are interested in using these meditations with groups, a simple method follows to serve as a guide. I'll use the service for Nancy and her baby to highlight certain key parts of this method that I have found helpful with groups. Feel free to modify it for the needs of your group. The method is also explained on the CD included with this book.

The Grace: At the beginning of Nancy's service we prayed for healing. It is helpful in a group to introduce the specific grace and theme of the gospel passage and meditation. A particular grace is suggested before each meditation in this book.

The Setting: Rather than immediately beginning with the meditation, we each prepared by remembering a loved one who had recently died. It is helpful to spend a short time creating a peaceful atmosphere before beginning the actual meditation. Quiet background music helps to do this.

The Story: Nancy shared her story with the group. In this book, a personal story precedes each meditation. The story reflects the grace for which we will be praying. The stories come from a wide range of people who, through their own faith lives, have attempted to take on the mind and values of Jesus. Their stories show how they have been transformed by the story, the person, and the dream of Jesus.

The Scripture: Javier then read the passage from the Gospel of Mark, which tells of Jesus healing Peter's mother-in-law. We connect our story to the story of Jesus. A Scripture passage precedes each meditation.

The Meditation: After asking the members of the group to close their eyes and use their imaginations to focus on the person for whom they were praying, we began reading the meditation in a slow, easy, flowing style.

The Anointing and Reflection: Because of her deep desire for healing, Nancy wanted to anoint the hands of each of us after the meditation. Nancy simply went around the group and traced oil in the shape of a cross on the palms of the hands of each person. This is a very powerful moment where touch and the scent of oil connect to a deep place within. Anointing is appropriate for each meditation, not only healing.

Before the meditation, when the group first came together, each of us had received a sheet of paper, which read, "Dear . . . , I miss you because. . . . " After Nancy had finished the anointing, we spent fifteen minutes writing a response and completing the statement "I miss you because." Each meditation in this book ends with questions for reflection and writing. The questions help people to focus their thoughts and reflections about what they just experienced in meditation.

The Sharing and Closing Prayer: Nancy took the candle from the middle of the circle, held it, and began to share what she had written. She then passed the candle to the next person to speak. That night in the chapel something powerful happened when each of us shared what we had written, connecting it to Jesus' story. (At the beginning of the meditation, it is good to remind the group about the importance of confidentiality so people can grow in trust and freedom together.)

Nancy closed the service with a prayer and we gave each other a sign of peace.

Summary of the Method

1. Introducing the grace to be asked for
2. Setting the mood
3. Reading a story
4. Reading the Scripture
5. The Meditation
6. Anointing and Reflection
7. Sharing and Closing Prayer

Many people like Krystal, Elias, and Rita have tried this method and have been transformed from within and without. I hope this method of gospel meditation helps you in your journey to know Jesus.

call

(Mark 1:14–20)

The Grace

To hear the ways Jesus calls me in my life and to be willing and courageous enough to answer yes to his call.

The Setting

The Story

Rob Smith is a businessman from Los Angeles. He serves as president of the Doheny Foundation, which supports Catholic works in the Los Angeles area, is involved in numerous other charitable works, and is well known in Los Angeles as a civic and church leader.

Many of us seek peace as the goal of our faith walk. We see peace as a comfortable state that we all desire. That's how I understood peace until a series of events in my faith journey led me to look at peace — and comfortability — in a new way.

Some years ago I attended a Cursillo retreat. The experience reinvigorated my prayer life and kindled my desire to walk more closely with Jesus. I started teaching religious education to sixth graders and made more time for rosaries, Mass, and spiritual reading. This part of my life became enriching — and comfortable. But this soon changed.

I was asked to take a group of teens to Skid Row to prepare and serve meals to the poor. In Los Angeles, where I live, as many as forty

thousand people live and sleep on the streets — hardly a comfortable situation. But for me serving the homeless would not be as convenient or comfortable as teaching religious education or going to Mass.

The kids finally wore me down, and I figured I could help them out by accompanying them. The poverty and hopelessness overwhelmed me. We started preparation of the meal at 7:30 a.m., served from 10:00 to 12:30, and cleaned until 1:30. As I worked, I couldn't stop thinking that Jesus taught and Jesus prayed, but Jesus was also there with the people. This part was not quite as easy — at least not for me. But as hard as I tried, I couldn't separate Jesus' being with people in need from the rest of his life and teachings. At first I wanted solutions to the homeless problem. Why, , I wondered, does this happen in a country so rich in people and resources? What can I do?

Then one day I took a tray, filled my bowl, and sat with those we served. I found people there instead of victims. We talked about our daily challenges, where we were from, the Dodgers, the shortage of restrooms in the area. Some had been in jail, some had lost jobs and family, and some struggled with addictive behaviors that led to homelessness. We shared instead of solved.

In these encounters, I became aware that these were people and not situations or problems simply to be solved. These were my brothers and sisters and not people to be treated with indifference. In the Beatitudes Jesus calls us to do more than seek his peace. He calls us to be peacemakers. And while this keeps me from ever being comfortable, it challenges me to become more whole.

— ROB SMITH

The Scripture

After John was arrested, Jesus went into Galilee and began preaching the Good News of God. He said, "The time has come; the kingdom of God is at hand. Change your ways and believe the Good News."

As Jesus was walking along the shore of Lake Galilee, he saw Simon and his brother Andrew casting a net in the lake, for they were fishermen. And Jesus said to them, "Follow me, and I will make you fishers of men." At once, they left their nets and followed him. Jesus went a little farther on and saw James and John, the sons of Zebedee; they were in their boat mending their nets. Immediately, Jesus called them and they followed him, leaving their father Zebedee in the boat with the hired men.

The Meditation

it was still dark
    above there were
    a few stars left
    most had disappeared
sitting
staring out
    at the breaking of small waves
    against the rocks
    the sound constant
thinking of the last night
    trying to fish
as i threw in
    the nets last night
i kept hearing jesus' words
    throw in the nets
    throw in your life
what was he talking about?
    i was happy with my life
    i was secure
    had a good family
    a good living
i could not wish for more
    throw in the nets
    throw in your life

i did not really know
what i was going to get
myself involved in
    when i started
    months ago
    to sit

and listen to jesus
as he talked to the people
now feel
we are becoming friends
but he is demanding
he doesn't settle for things
to be mediocre
throw in the nets
throw in your life
thinking of these words
as they flowed
through my mind
again and again
trying to enter my heart

suddenly felt
the presence of jesus
next to me
it was still dark
but i could tell
the day was struggling
to make an appearance
jesus greeted me
i was surprised
by this appearance
remember the moment
as if it were yesterday

he looks at me
are you ready peter
to throw in your nets?
to throw in your life?
are you ready?
are you ready to follow me?
am i ready to throw in the nets?
to find out what they bring
by following you jesus?

felt great emotion
at this moment
thinking of my life
of my security
to follow you?
to go with you?
what would that mean?
know my life
would be totally different
reflecting
listening to the waves
feeling
the dawn
come upon us

jesus
during this last month
i have spent time with you
have watched you carefully
know
when someone speaks
from the heart
speaks
from a place of truth
or is fooling the people
during these years
here in this village
we have had
so many false leaders
i know the condition
of our people
i have been seeking someone
who can help us
i walk home after fishing
think and think
want to do something

but have never known
how to do it

jesus
        since i have known you
        i feel
        i could one day be moved
to throw my nets in
        with you
not too sure
        what will happen
at the depths
you will bring me to
        but even now
        just sitting here with you
                there is something
                happening within my heart

peter
        i need to go
        to another village
        i need to be there by noon
        will you come with me?
here was the moment
        i looked at jesus
        into his eyes
        they were serious
        they were inviting
looking inside myself
        knew if i said yes
        there was no turning back
the nets would be thrown
        in forever
        but i was feeling something else
        that was giving me the strength
        to say yes
i was feeling a love strong

flowing through my heart
watching the sun now appear
 over the mountains
 in the background
watching the birds
diving in and out
of the water
feeling that a love
was drawing me

 i said in a voice
 that came from
 a very deep place
yes jesus
 i will go with you now
 know where that village is
 know the problems
 they are having
it is going to be challenging
to be there

i had said yes
 the sun was coming up higher
 over the mountains
yes
 i never retreated
 having said those words
 that left my mouth
could feel jesus
 was happy
i had said yes
his face lit up
 after i said that simple word
yes
 was glad i would be able
 to help this one
was moved that

he wanted me
to be part of his group

we began walking along
the shore
    leaving the nets folded
feeling
as if bigger nets
had been thrown
into this lake
i was not too sure
what was going to happen
    that day
we went to the village
    after that our group traveled
    every day together
met many people
some who were suffering
greatly
    i learned so much
    from jesus
    after saying yes
i really never understood
what that would mean
just like
i never know
never fully know
what i will be doing
in the future

now looking back
    after all these years
now sitting at this spot
    here at the lake
    where jesus
    asked me this question
    when i said yes

what i am feeling
   is gratitude
never did i think
    it would be possible
    to have my life filled
    with so many powerful experiences
it was not easy
    there were constant pressures
    there were constant conflicts
it was not a problem-free life
but what happened
now looking back
during these years
    is i am grateful
    i can see the faces
    of the people
    that were part of our group
jesus drew them in
tried to explain
    his message
it always seemed
    we really never understood
    the full meaning of his message
sometimes it seemed
that everyone
    was grasping it
    but it was so challenging
i think that some
did not want to understand
because
they would have to change
i think back
to the people
    i have met
to the healings
the spiritual moments

the times
> when jesus left me
> on my own
>> the insecurity i felt
>> at first
> here i was a fisherman
> and i was dealing
> with matters
> that confounded the mind
> the complexity
> the degree of anguish
> that the people suffer

i was glad
that i was given
the opportunity
> to walk with jesus
i never have forgotten
the simple word
yes
> that i said
> at this spot

The Anointing and Reflection

1. Did I ever say yes to a call? What was that time? What excited me about the call? What scared me about the call?

2. In looking back at the answer to a call, how do I feel about my choice?

3. How do I continue to say yes? How do I hold back or say no?

The Sharing and Closing Prayer

 friends

(John 1:35–39)

The Grace

To know Jesus at a deeper level, from the heart, and to be filled with a desire to follow him.

The Setting

The Story

Oscar Galindo is from Los Angeles and is serving a life sentence at Pelican Bay State Prison in Northern California. He began meditation classes at Central Juvenile Hall in Los Angeles when he was sixteen years old.

Reflecting on this meditation reminds me of the sacred friendship I've found in Jesus, a friendship found in no other person. Before this bond with Jesus, my life was a dream. I had grown up ignoring God's presence in my life. As far as I knew, God and Jesus were only words people used. Living my short life to its fullest limits, I experienced dangers — life-threatening moments, situations where anything could have happened — along with the good times and bad. Somehow I always survived. I'd always had a weird feeling within me. I always told myself it was only adrenaline.

I remember the person I was. It's as if I had billions of evil spirits in me. Life was a game, a dream. I blinded myself to the truth by deceiving myself about life. It was my world, after all. My soul was hidden by the dark midnight fog of demons surrounding it. I allowed my anger

and hatred to run my life. Yet throughout my youth something always seemed wrong. I was missing something.

Finally, at the end of my teens, I began to notice Jesus. There was something in hearing about him and learning of his teachings and his ways that kept my curiosity open. In time, changes began to take place in me. I began to pray just as I had seen others pray, but wondered if it was working. Was I talking to myself or was someone actually listening? The day came when I wanted to change my life. What was I looking for? I had always wanted a peaceful life. Yet I always chose to walk down the dark alleys of life, often finding myself in places I truly did not want to be. I wanted out. I want to quit my addiction to my old life. But if I did that, what would be next?

What was next was my new life. I've come to know Jesus, and I've realized that it's been his presence I've been ignoring while convincing myself that it was only my adrenaline. The new life in him, and him in me, has changed the feeling of weirdness I once experienced. Jesus became my friend — the One who knows me best and is at my side, the One who has never forsaken me and has guided me through the battles of life to reach the light at the end of the darkness.

— OSCAR GALINDO

The Scripture

On the following day John was standing there again with two of his disciples. As Jesus walked by, John looked at him and said, "There is the Lamb of God." On hearing this, the two disciples followed Jesus. He turned and saw them following, and he said to them, "What are you looking for?" They answered, "Rabbi (which means Master), where are you staying?" Jesus said, "Come and see." So they went and saw where he stayed and spent the rest of that day with him. It was about four o'clock in the afternoon.

The Meditation

the water is sparkling
in spite of so many people
nearby
there is a solitude deep

so the baptist tells us
    to follow the one
    walking in front

i stare into the river
    watching as it winds
    along the curves of the land
there is a stillness
about this afternoon
    it is as if you can feel
    something deeper happening
it is as if somehow you can
be brought into what is inside
at the deepest core
    where most of the time
    we never go

taking my gaze
    away from the river
    from the sparkling
    on the water
    away from the steady flow

in the distance
    this one stops and sits
    watching all the people
    around him
he also is enjoying the afternoon
not hurrying
feeling the flow
    of the moment

feeling something deeper happening
    know i will soon
    need to introduce myself

he starts to walk again
looking at him

as he passes
    underneath the tallest trees
    as he passes through the shade
i have this tremendous desire
to tell him
that i have lately been trying
    so hard to do
    something for our country
i feel this strong desire
    to talk to him
    about the last five years
how hard i have tried
to find others
    who will be willing to risk
it always seems the same
how no one seems interested
    and here i am
    leaving the baptist
    from whom i have learned
    so much
when would this journey ever end?
when would i ever be able
to find what i was looking for?

he moves from underneath the shade
    turning away from the river
i watch him
as he makes the turn
    on the path
i still cannot make out
    his face
all i can see is his white robe
    flowing
as the breeze blows against me
as he starts to ascend the incline
asking myself

should i continue
to follow him
or go back to the baptist?
something within me
pushes me
to also make the turn
away from the familiar
away from what i know
to make the turn
to meet someone
different
now walking along the path

reflecting as i take
each step
how i never know
what is going to happen
when i listen
to what is happening inside
always being thrown off course
always finding myself
walking down paths
i never thought
i would be walking

once again he sits down
looking
at the riverbed below
he sees us
walking behind him
know
i need to come closer
know
there is no turning back
it is time
to introduce ourselves
quickly approaching him

he stands up
    i look into his face

he greets me
    can i help you?
    what are you looking for?

    what am i looking for?
this search is why
i left the baptist
that is why i have taken
    so many risks
that is why
i have been looking so hard
for someone
who also has a vision
    what am i looking for?

i don't know
why i said it
but i could not think
of anything else to say
    where do you live?
so there it was

he says
    come and see
    i live over those hills
        would you like
        to see a different part
        of this land?
    come let us walk
so this one
whom i had never met before
was inviting me
    to come
    to see
where he lives

why would i want
        to walk with him
        to see where he lives?
but once again
there was this deep desire
        to share with him
        what i had been experiencing
        in our country
was not too sure
why i said it
but i did
        about why i like to live
        in my village
        what had happened during the years
        to the poor of our village

could see he was interested
        in what i was saying
we walked and walked
talking
        about many things
        about so many events
        in our lives
he asks
        why i wanted
        to follow the baptist
i tell him

i know he understands
he wants to know
        what was the hardest challenge
        working with the people
        what was the best part of it
        during these last months
telling him
makes a difference
        somehow just by telling him

there is something different
within me

arriving at his house
passing through the doors
    feeling
    that something new is happening
that i will never be the same
just like i felt
at the river
    know something deeper is happening
sitting around his table
we begin to speak
    about more of our lives
    can tell him anything
as the afternoon passes
    into night
as we pass the hours
talking
    feel how important
    to have found someone
    who understands
    what i am saying
how important
    not to keep so much
    enclosed within
a beginning that afternoon
    of sharing what is within
    with this one
offering his friendship
which i know
    will deepen with the passing
know this time
      i found
      the one
    i had been looking for

The Anointing and Reflection

1. Has there ever been a time when something within pushed me to turn away from the familiar, to meet someone different? What do I remember about that time? Did I allow myself to be pushed? What came of that decision?

2. Who are my friends? Do I feel understood by them? Are there joys, hurts, or concerns I keep enclosed within?

3. How do I talk with Jesus? Do I feel understood? What would it be like to talk with Jesus about the joys, hurts, and concerns enclosed within?

The Sharing and Closing Prayer

morning  prayer

(Mark 1:29–39)

The Grace

To open my heart and mind to God more freely and to increase my desire to turn to God in prayer.

The Setting

The Story

Frank Montejano has long been involved in Catholic education. He is a regional supervisor of elementary schools for the Archdiocese of Los Angeles and has served as principal at Blessed Sacrament Parish in Hollywood and Our Lady of Guadalupe in East Los Angeles.

Every morning after the bell to begin school rang, we prayed. It is that way with most Catholic schools, and no different for us at Blessed Sacrament. Here — along Sunset Boulevard in Hollywood, amid street people and prostitutes — we prayed for family, friends, the homeless, the outcasts. But one day, Heather, an eighth-grader, in her last weeks before graduating, approached me just as the morning bell rang. She looked very distressed as she made a request. "Can we especially pray this morning for my mother?" she asked. Her mother, she explained, was seriously ill and having major surgery that morning. Tears streamed down Heather's face as she recounted the various doctors her mother had visited and all the times her mother had been to the hospital.

This surgery would be her mother's last chance. I couldn't remember Heather, reticent and soft-spoken, ever asking for anything. This was probably the longest conversation we had in the years I'd known her. But here she was asking for our prayers — for her mother.

I moved to the loudspeaker and asked all who were present that morning — students, teachers, some parents — to pray for Heather's mother, whose story I shared. And as we prayed, three hundred strong, five-year-olds and grandparents and everything in between, I glanced at Heather, her face now washed with calm as her friends, her faith community — some known, most unknown — prayed in unison to our God for help. Something happened as we prayed. Our prayer was real, not rote. Heather felt it, and I felt it too. I went to sleep that evening with the image of Heather's face as we all prayed. It was a look of serenity, of one who knew that the prayers of the people she loved were what counted most — and that these prayers would be the difference, if there was going to be a difference.

The next morning at school I looked for Heather, and she looked for me. How did it go? Again, her face told the story — joy! Heather could barely contain herself. She threw her arms around me and said that it was our prayers that did it. The surgery was a success. "Can you thank the students for their prayers?" she asked. "Of course," I said. "Of course."

— FRANK MONTEJANO

The Scripture

On leaving the synagogue, Jesus went to the home of Simon and Andrew with James and John. As Simon's mother-in-law was sick in bed with fever, they immediately told him about her. Jesus went to her and taking her by the hand, raised her up. The fever left her and she began to wait on them. That evening at sundown, people brought to Jesus all the sick and those who had evil spirits: the whole town was pressing around the door. Jesus healed many who had various diseases, and drove out many demons; but he did not let them speak, for they knew who he was.

Very early in the morning, before daylight, Jesus went off to a lonely place where he prayed. Simon and the others went out, too, searching for him; and

*when they found him they said, "Everyone is looking for you." Then Jesus
answered, "Let's go to the nearby villages so that I may preach there too; for
that is why I came."*

*So Jesus set out to preach in all the synagogues throughout Galilee; he
also cast out demons.*

The Meditation

it was early morning
the stars still
present
jesus
    had tossed and turned
    all night
    thinking
    of what had passed
    through him
    during the day
it was 4:00 a.m.
jesus sat up
    in his bed
    listening
    to the silence
    of early morning
felt full of faces
    full of events
    during this last day
    full of memories
jesus knew
    he wanted to go
    down by the lake
    before everyone else rose
walking slowly
    down the path
    that led to the shore
reflecting

    on stories of women
    in a nearby village
    the suffering their lives contained
jesus
    had been moved
    by listening to them
    their pain entered into him
    whirled around
    so fast during the night
    that he needed
    to let some of it out
    release the intensity
    by the water
jesus looking up
at the stars
feeling the vastness
of the universe
jesus
arriving at the shore
    of the lake
he knew
    far out
    the fishermen were
    making their way back
for the present
there was no one
only company
    was the profound silence
    of the early morning
jesus
    in the stillness
    in the darkness
sat down
along the shore
    praying
    abba

i have come here
this morning
because i want
to let your presence
fill me
it has been so hard
as of late
as i walked yesterday
a group followed me
their children were sick
they wanted me
to lay hands on them
the tears
and the anguish
of the mothers
            moved me

abba

i needed to be
at the village
but i could not leave
        that group
i laid my hands
on the heads
of those small ones
your light abba
flowed through me
into those ones
now cured

abba
i know you understand
what i am saying
        yesterday very quickly
there was a whole
hillside of requests
filling every empty space

abba
    i know you understand
    more than anyone else
    when i tell you
        this early morning
        i wanted to run
abba
    felt drained
        exhausted
        and even empty
abba
    the one i love
    that is why
    i have come here
    i don't want
        to feel overwhelmed
        don't want to
abba
    i look out
        into the distance
        i know
        there are many fishing boats
        returning
        but i see nothing
abba
    sometimes
    i don't feel you close
    i know
        you cannot solve all this
        for me
    i have just come here
        to sit with you awhile
    to tell you
        what has been happening to me
        because
        i know you care

abba
> i find when i am with you
> i have the strength
>> to return
>> to work

abba
> tears streaming down
>> that leper
>> who approached me
>> yesterday
>> who was so disfigured
> remaining in silence

abba
> sometimes
> the suffering
>> of our people
>> is so great

jesus
feeling his abba
close
very present
in this moment

abba
> yesterday afternoon
> i passed through the center
> of the village
> naomi ran out
> of her house
> she told me
> how the night before
> four roman soldiers
> had bound her son
> for plotting
> to overthrow their power
>> she asked me
>> to help her

abba
    i felt so powerless
        so weak
    walking through those garrison doors
        to downstairs
    walking into the cell
    where they had beaten
        joshua

more tears streaming
down jesus' face
    as he told his abba
    the cruelty of the empire
how the youth
of the country
    were being annihilated
    by a fearful monster

jesus
peering out
into the darkness
reflecting
    on how so much injustice
    is so cruel
    how it destroys
    so much human life
as jesus
sat praying
with his abba
something began
to happen

once again
everything made sense

jesus felt
    deep union
    closeness

that morning
by the lake
in the early dawn

once again
everything made sense

The Anointing and Reflection

1. Do I need silence in my life? How do I find silence if I need it?
   Do I experience God in the silence?

2. Have I experienced a close connection with Abba?

3. Can I remember an experience of prayer in which everything
   made sense? How did I feel? Where was God in that moment?
   What was my connection to God in that moment?

The Sharing and Closing Prayer

possessed

(Mark 1:21–28)

The Grace

To understand the things in my life that control me, that lead me to sin, and to let go of them and allow Jesus to heal and transform me.

The Setting

The Story

Bill Garcia works with the Los Angeles County Department of Children and Family Services. He also facilitates group therapy and provides alcohol and drug instruction for both self-referred and court-mandated individuals struggling with substance abuse.

On a beautiful, sunny Sunday morning, I was coming to, awakened from a night of drinking. The house was empty. I was divorced. The children had left with their mother, and I believed that I was alone. I was in a deplorable physical state due to my drinking. Feelings of uselessness and self-pity had a hold on me, feelings of emptiness and a deep hole full of loneliness. The feelings were very real. The devil himself was embracing me. He had such a strong hold. The darkness was so deep. I had never felt so hopeless, so lonely, such true despair.

Addiction — what had happened to me? An average kid with worldly dreams fulfilled. I had a good profession, family, friends, and many worldly possessions. I had always known of a God, but he seemed so far away, so distant. God was "out there" to me. Alcohol slowly became my friend. My addiction seduced me slowly; it was fun for many

years. It relaxed me, relieved my stress, and made me more sociable. My addiction progressed, and I continued on a torturous path of destruction. The inner feelings of darkness and loneliness deepened; the devil was ever so close.

I had many moments and thoughts of stopping, and I made many vain attempts to stop. Self-will could not stop me.

This Sunday morning would change my life forever. My usual routine was to wake up, shaking, then take a drink to ease the nerves. This morning I didn't drink. I lay helpless and asked God, as I had never asked before, for help. I know now that I touched Jesus within me that morning. Jesus himself cast out that demon within me. I found my Abba, my Daddy, within me that morning. Through his mercy and compassion, he got me through that day and has continued to shed his loving grace for all the years since then. That morning I found a loving power within me, Jesus himself, and he led me to begin the process of recovery.

There is hope for the hopeless amid deep darkness and despair. Addiction. It was there that I found, within me, this loving Jesus. Jesus, this loving power who cast out demons, is not "out there," but within.

— BILL GARCIA

The Scripture

They went into the town of Capernaum and Jesus began to teach in the synagogue during the sabbath assemblies. The people were astonished at the way he taught, for he spoke as one having authority and not like the teachers of the Law.

It happened that a man with an evil spirit was in their synagogue and he shouted, "What do you want with us, Jesus of Nazareth? Have you come to destroy us? I know who you are: You are the Holy One of God." Then Jesus faced him and said with authority, "Be silent and come out of this man!" The evil spirit shook the man violently and, with a loud shriek, came out of him.

All the people were astonished and they wondered, "What is this? With what authority he preaches! He even orders evil spirits and they obey him!" And Jesus' fame spread throughout all the country of Galilee.

The Meditation

in the early morning
    i had gone down
    by the water
    to be with
    my abba
it was dark
there was a silence
at that time of day
reflecting during these days
    on all
    the possessed of capernaum
    some wanted to change
abba
sometimes i wonder
    where you are
    when i listen
    to the stories
    of these ones
it is like a dark cloud
that has taken over their hearts
    they live
    but it is not like
    they are really living
yesterday afternoon
    as the sun was setting
a man came to where
    i was speaking
    i could see his heart
he began to speak
i was sad abba
i saw the heart of this one
    how he treated his wife
    the blows to her
i could see abba

the faces of his children
inside of his heart
and i felt sad
seeing such potential
but he was never in the home
and they were young
they needed a father
they needed a father
so much
i felt powerless
when he came to talk
his heart was surrounded
by a dark cloud
how many people
in this country have i met
whose hearts
have been taken
over by this darkness?
before i could say anything
he ran off
because he knew
i could read his heart
sitting here with you abba
i pray for this man
i pray for all who are possessed
like he is
there is such darkness within
that to kill another
would mean nothing to him
what do you do
when you are in front
of those whose hearts are cold?
looking out at the lake
as it was changing colors
changing colors
feeling a sadness

sweep through me
just as the wind off the lake
was sweeping across the water
it was now time
to walk back into the village
to begin another day
wandering up to the synagogue
    to be free
        not to be ruled
        by any powers
        that want to rule
        over the heart
thinking
    of how easy
    it is to sell the heart
    to give it away
    for something that will not last
the unhappiness that comes
from selling your heart
how important
to keep the heart free
    to be full of light and love
    to avoid
    the powers that drive so many
    to action
    that fill others
    with darkness

seeing my friends we began
    to walk toward the synagogue
it was a beautiful day
    the sun was out now
    it was warm
you could look down
from the synagogue
and see the lake below

i was still thinking
      of the man i met yesterday
   to be possessed by such darkness
   and did he even want to change
   to cast off the power
   that had control of his heart?
the look in his eyes
   still haunts me
what happened
that he could breathe in
so much darkness?
i was glad that i could come
    here and listen to the word
    listen to the voice of my abba
the synagogue was inviting
this morning
   wanted to get away
   from this darkness

we walked in through large doors
this place to reflect
   on what was happening
   inside and outside
we walked through the doors
   were making our way
   to sit
when the same man
who came to me yesterday
sees me
i feel shocked to find him
here
but it is clear
he is looking for me
he falls on his knees
   jesus i implore you
   i beg you

after i talked with you yesterday
i could not sleep all last night
i feel as if i am drowning
i want to rid myself
of this darkness
    but i have no control over it
    it has taken me over
    the first thing i did last night
    after seeing you
    was to become intoxicated
    i didn't want this
i promised my family
    i would not do this
when i got home
i saw the faces
of my children
they were hungry
they wanted my attention
but i left the house

there was a stillness
within the synagogue
    no one was moving
    not one sound
the man was screaming for help
i remembered back
to the time
with my abba in the morning
in a strong voice
i loudly commanded
    the darkness controlling his heart
    to leave
all of a sudden
as a dark presence escaped
into the synagogue
a real change

of temperature was felt
the man lay on the ground
totally exhausted
  i went over
  picked him up
this time
he did not try to run away
he had let go
of this darkness
possessing him
his heart was free again
lines of gratitude
spread across
his once very troubled face
  thank you jesus
  for taking away this evil
  that i had chosen
i felt powerless
  to free myself
yesterday when i talked to you
i wanted to free myself
  but i was not ready
never again
do i want to go back
to how i was
possessed by powers of death

he walked out the door
of the synagogue
free
he walked to go to his house
he became
  the husband he never was
he became
  the father he never was
he always remembered

back to that morning
in the synagogue
    when this one freed him
    from the darkness
he never missed
going to the synagogue
to thank god
for this healing

The Anointing and Reflection

1. What darkness lives within me? How does it affect my life and the lives of those around me?

2. Do I want to let go of this darkness? Can I let go of the darkness? Do I have the courage to let Jesus' healing light into the darkness?

3. Have I ever experienced a release from a dark presence? Can I help others to be released from their darkness?

The Sharing and Closing Prayer

 healed

(Mark 1:29–34)

The Grace

To be healed in all the areas of my life that need healing and, in turn, to have the courage and desire to bring God's healing to others.

The Setting

The Story

Laura Clark lives in Los Angeles. She has been serving as a volunteer in numerous organizations for several years.

Tonight at Juvenile Hall Nicole sat in our meditation circle. As we went around the group in the opening minutes of the session, she shared her thoughts about the week. She said she has been feeling much better and having a pretty good week because of something that happened during her visit with her father on Sunday. She had attended the retreat on Saturday, and one of the writing exercises had asked, "How do you feel when you see your mom in court?" (Nicole's primary caretaker has been her father, so she changed the word from "mom" to "dad" and answered the question.) She said that she knew, as soon as she started to write, that all her feelings about her dad's support were coming to the surface, and she wrote her response as a sort of letter to him. Another question asked, "What's the hardest thing about your life right now?" Nicole expressed how she felt about the pain her mistakes have brought to her dad.

Many others probably felt and wrote along those same lines. What is special and impressive about Nicole is how she used her writing as a

tool for healing between herself and her father. She talked of how she hadn't been able to tell her dad, in person, the things she had written. She had kept her feelings to herself because she did not know how to begin talking to him. But with her paper in hand, she had the courage to read the questions and the answers she'd written aloud to him as he sat across from her. Her father cried as she read.

Nicole smiled broadly as she said she feels "better and not so heavy" since then. This is certainly among the most beautiful stories I've heard from a kid since I began volunteering a year and half ago. Who knows if, or when, this important healing moment between Nicole and her dad would have happened without the retreat.

— LAURA CLARK

The Scripture

On leaving the synagogue, Jesus went to the home of Simon and Andrew with James and John. As Simon's mother-in-law was sick in bed with fever, they immediately told him about her. Jesus went to her and taking her by the hand, raised her up. The fever left her and she began to wait on them. That evening at sundown, people brought to Jesus all the sick and those who had evil spirits: the whole town was pressing around the door. Jesus healed many who had various diseases, and drove out many demons; but he did not let them speak, for they knew who he was.

The Meditation

> i was waiting
> outside of peter's house
> waiting
> i had been crippled
>   all my life
>   i had been paralyzed
>   since birth
> i looked about me
>   i saw a sea of faces
>   many of these people
>   i had known since childhood

looking back
at the lake
the light was barely shining
    over its surface

to be healed

so many people
had spoken
about jesus
how he could touch you
    you would feel
    a burning sensation
god's power
would be flowing through you

looked
inside peter's house
saw jesus peering out
he saw this line of sick
he looked moved
knew soon
    he would leave those doors
    and begin to heal

jesus leaving peter's house
    he saw me
    he came over
    to where i was
    he bent down
    he looked at my crippled legs
jesus put his hands on top
of my legs
feeling power
flow into them
    i was no longer confined
    to such a locked up position
    rather my legs were straightening

jesus looked at me saying
    samuel
    come with me
    i need you to help me
    to heal
    all these people
    it is too much for me

jesus i have been crippled
    all my life
i have never been to school
don't know anything
about healing

samuel come with me

we walked down
    the long line of sick
to be walking
not to be in pain
to be whole
    there was a joy
    that flowed through my heart
    walking again
i wanted to run
now jesus
was asking me
    to heal

there was an elderly woman
    her skin disease
    was horrible
i almost
felt like crying right there
i felt so helpless

jesus looked at me
    thought to myself

who is this person?
first he heals me
then he asks me
to come with him to heal

everything was happening so fast
he knelt next to this woman
she mumbled some words
could not understand them

jesus
looking at me
now put your hands
over her head
ask god
to let healing
flow through into her
took my hands
put them over her head
looking at the sad expression
in her eyes
i closed my eyes
with my whole heart
i prayed
god
i am no one
to be asking you this
since i myself
have just been healed
but god
i ask for my sister here
she is suffering so much
i know you do not wish her
to suffer so much
i ask you
to heal her

with those words
    heal her
it was as if an explosion
had occurred
it was as if
something broke open
it was like
a brilliant light
in front
hearing again and again
    heal her

god
    heal her
    heal her
i could feel tears streaming
    down her face
felt a power
    flow through my hands
    into her
felt something
powerful was happening

i slowly
opened my eyes
    looked
    in front of me
she did not have
    blotches of red oozing sores
    her skin was clean
i looked at jesus
    he was smiling
once again
    could not figure out
    what was happening
to be a channel
    of his healing power

i was glad
i could be part
   of this healing

the young boy
next to her
reached out his arm
to me
   help me he cried
   my head hurts
   so much
   day and night
      help me
looked back
   at jesus
   but he was helping
   someone else
i knew
   could not leave
   this young one
   alone
   without trying to help him
i knelt down
   next to him
   he told me his name
   was joshua
   he was nine

   i just hurt
   please help me
   please help
   so this pain can go away
   i hurt so much

large tears rolled down
his face
our country

has so much pain
so much suffering
    joshua...
i could not finish
what i was going to say
instead
i just put my hands
    over his head
my heart
was moved so deeply
feeling his head
beneath my hands
    i desire so much
    to be able to help him
closing my eyes
once again
praying with all my heart

god
        i feel powerless
        i know you do not want
        the young to have to suffer
        so much
      i am asking you
        to heal
        joshua
        please help him
        to be whole
        once again

it was as if a loud explosion
      as a rush of power
      flowed
      into this young boy's body
flowing through my hands
as if lightning broke
into the moment

light
heat
could tell healing
had taken place within joshua
    his eyes opened
    a joy spread across his face
he jumped up
    hugged me
    wild with joy
he knew that his life
was going to be different
    not to have to suffer
    so intensely

so i came here today
to be touched by josus
    he did touch heal me
but never did i think
that he would ask me
    to do the same

before
    i could reflect anymore
a young mother
came before me
    with her baby
    who appeared half dead
    burning with a fever
her weak infant's body
struggling to survive
the mother looked
me in the eyes
imploring me
to help her baby
    please
    i have already lost two children
        from diseases

        please help me
        my baby's name is rafael

once again i tried
        put my hands
        over the baby's head
once again
        god's healing
        passed through me
        into this new life
well into the evening
i knelt down again and again
healing light
flowing through me
praying
with my whole heart
        for god's power
        to continue to flow
i do not remember
        how many people
        there were on that hillside
i was just moved deeply
        by the pain
        the suffering
        of so many

it was late
        into the night
when there
was no one left
i saw jesus
he was
        sitting
        staring looking down
        at the lake
        lit up
        by the moon strong

i joined him
    we walked down to the lake
    could not ask one question
we walked
without saying a word
being involved
in the mystery of healing
    of bringing wholeness
    where there is brokenness
reaching the shore
sitting down
listening to the water
    beat against the shore
    again and again

Jesus
i never had experienced healing
    till this afternoon
first you touch heal me
then you ask me to help you
    to heal others
i am grateful
    to be a channel
    of this healing
i saw so many people
all evening
    who were in pain
    the old the young
you were with me
giving me strength
    to heal
i do not even know
what happened
except
that i am grateful
    that you asked me

to do this work
of being a healer
feel humbled jesus
to be a healer

after that day
i would accompany jesus
i was no longer crippled
no longer shriveled up
i enjoyed this healing work
in the countryside

with jesus and his friends
after that afternoon
jesus
asked me many times
to help him
each time
every time
i felt insecure
i could not do it
it was too much
there was too much suffering
i felt this every time
jesus asked me
but every time
i began
every time
i knelt down
laid hands
praying
for god's healing
there was a change
a transformation
that afternoon
changed my life
i knew

the power of healing
knew how much
our god
    desires us
    to be whole
how important
to go before god
    to ask him
    for this healing

The Anointing and Reflection

1. What healing do I desire? Can I ask Jesus for healing?

2. How am I a channel for healing? How does Jesus' healing power flow through me?

3. In what ways do I prevent the flow of healing power?

The Sharing and Closing Prayer

martha

(Luke 10:38–42)

The Grace

To trust the deepest desires of my heart.

The Setting

The Story

Dick Howard is the director of campus ministry at Archbishop Mitty High School in San Jose, California.

My eighty-four-year-old mother can't hear very well. At times she jokes that she belongs to the "What?" club because without her hearing aid (and sometimes with it), "What?" is the first word she says when someone speaks to her. I know that not being able to hear very well bothers her because, among other things, she is well aware that my wife and I occasionally have to make an extra effort for her to hear us.

However, my mother's hearing difficulty does not in the least affect her ability to love and care for other people. Whenever we are out and someone asks for money for some cause or simply for food, she stops and reaches into her purse for a donation. At restaurants, she always calls the bus persons over and makes sure they get their own tip. Whenever any of her children, grandchildren, great-grandchildren, or anyone she hears about needs something, she is there without reservation, ready to help. Although she speaks no Spanish, she communicates clearly with her Spanish-speaking grandchildren from El Salvador.

The key is that my mother makes time for people. She touches them

76

physically in her loving hugs and emotionally with her enormous open heart. Like Jesus, she doesn't want people to see it as a big deal, or even to know about it. She just does it. She hears things on a deeper level. She hears people's hearts.

Jesus challenges us to make time to be with people, to listen to them, to heal with our love and care, and to avoid making a big deal about it. All of us have difficulties we bring to this challenge, whether they be physical, mental, or emotional. But these challenges don't have to get in the way. A hard-of-hearing, diabetic, eighty-four-year-old great-grandmother is proof enough of that to me.

— DICK HOWARD

The Scripture

As Jesus and his disciples were on their way, he entered a village and a woman called Martha welcomed him to her house. She had a sister named Mary who sat down at the Lord's feet to listen to his words. Martha, meanwhile, was busy with all the serving and finally she said, "Lord, don't you care that my sister has left me to do all the serving?"

But the Lord answered, "Martha, Martha, you worry and are troubled about many things, whereas only one thing is needed. Mary has chosen the better part, and it will not be taken away from her."

The Meditation

the room was full of papers
        piled high
from the window you could look
down to the street

what am i doing?
        this is the question
        i am asking myself
        this morning
as i stare at the work
        before me
it always seems

there is too much to do
not enough time

last night
i walked around the plaza
    leisurely enjoying
    the night air
i walked
    i did not run
this morning i am rushing
once again
last night was a good reminder
    that life can be different
    does not have
    to go so fast
i begin to think
about all i have to accomplish
    this day
as i do this
voices outside
    my window
    catch my attention
i recognize the voice
of jesus and his friends

i look about me
i feel so trapped
on one hand i am so happy
    that jesus and his disciples
    are visiting
but on the other hand
    i feel the pressure
    of how many things
    i still need to do
rushing downstairs
    opening the front door
    there they are

now looking
into jesus' face

jesus smiling
    martha good to see you
he has his traveling bag
around his shoulder
he is glad to come inside
proceeding
    to the coolest room
thinking to myself
    of all the things
    i need to do
as i reflect on this
my sister mary
enters
goes to jesus
she sits
begins a conversation
they begin to talk
    about the happenings
    around this village
    the recent captures
    and killings
then mary begins
    to talk about her life

i want to stay
and listen to what jesus
tells her
but my sense of obligation
    pulls me
    to the kitchen
beginning to
cut the vegetables
prepare the meat
as i do this

i feel resentful
    and sad
at the same time
i so much want
to be there with jesus
how to better plan my day?
or what do i do
that i never
can just sit
    down and enjoy
    the company of friends?

as i chop and chop
reflecting
how true that is
just to have had time to walk
rather than run
to experience what i did
    last night in the plaza
no one is forcing me
    to be different
no one forced me
    to come back here
i could have stayed with jesus
but i didn't

to go slower
to enjoy life
always running
with my desk piled up

tears begin
to fall quickly
from my eyes
did not realize
how i am victim
to my own compulsions

i would like to change
know that as
i continue to cook
know that i want
    to do less
    to be more present
    to enjoy life more
what is happening to my life?
do i just go through
the motions of the day?
    to go slower
    to do less
    and i will do more
to reach
    the absolute silence
    that is within

start to cut the bread
watching the knife
pierce into the loaf
remembering
whenever
    i would take time out
in the morning
and i would sit
    in the darkness
of the dawn
outside in the back
    there was a stillness
a silence
a peace
that penetrated my whole being
    it would change my whole day
but i have not done that
    for many days
my spirit

yearning
for deeper union

as i start to move
the food to the table
    to lead a more simple life
    where life is different
    is not so full
finish the last preparations
sweat mixing together
with my deep emotions
walk back into the room
    there is a peacefulness
    a tranquility
which seems the opposite
of who i am
ready to open my mouth
    and announce
    that the food is ready
but nothing comes out
rather i feel pulled
to sit down next to jesus

when the group finishes speaking
    jesus smiles
    asks me
    what i am thinking

jesus
    i sit here
    next to you
you have been here many times
in our house
each time you come
i find myself
    involved in so many tasks
    always busy about something

i fill up my day
with so many nonessential tasks
i would like to change

jesus looking me in the eyes
        martha would you really
                like to change?

yes jesus

i follow jesus out the door
he tells the group
he wants to speak with me
we wander over to the plaza
jesus asks me
what i have been doing lately

i tell him
        how i am involved
        in a project
        to help with the orphanage
jesus i like to do this
        it gives me life
i start to get excited
i can tell jesus is interested
        in what i say
he cares about how i feel
he asks me questions
just walking around the plaza
        not hurrying
so martha
do you want
        to let go
        of some things
        that are not essential?
        it will be difficult at first
walking around the plaza
watching the children play

the oldest
    sitting on the benches
        content
        not to have to do anything
we sit on a wooden bench
and i tell jesus
    what is inside me
    about my desires
    my dreams
sitting on this bench
speaking about those dreams
will never forget this afternoon
as the day cools off
as the afternoon is ending
    dream of what life
    could be like
just feels good to be here
not having to do anything
to accomplish anything
so different from how
    i began the day
telling jesus
    about the people
    in my life who are important
why is something happening within
    doing this?
somehow
it is making a difference
    telling jesus
        about the pain
            i am having in relationships
        the anxiety of not having
        the money to cover expenses
i can tell
    jesus
    is glad to be here with me

he begins to talk
        about his days of late
i can tell life is not easy
for him either
he also is glad
to be able to tell me
        about himself
feel alive in my heart
a very different feeling
from the anger
        i was feeling
        in the kitchen
rather feel a burning great
        for this one

jesus
i don't want to waste my life
that is my greatest fear
that is why sometimes
        i cannot stop
this country
is so unjust
sometimes i cannot sleep
        at night
thinking about what i have seen
want to do so much
feel so powerless
so weak
that is why i go in circles
but jesus
i just know that
        being overloaded
        does not achieve
        what i am supposed to do
would like to do something
to make this a better world

would like to do so many things
and just sitting
    here with you jesus
realize there is
    only one thing important
    only one thing important
to do all from the love
that is found in the heart
    to do all this with love
realize jesus
if i would only listen
    to this love
    in my heart more
i would know
what to do

as the sun
sets this afternoon
i learn something
that i will never forget
i go back to it
    again and again
being with jesus
doing nothing
everything
    begins to happen

The Anointing and Reflection

1. Is my desk piled high with things to do? Am I involved with too many good things? Are there nonessential projects and tasks that I can let go of?

2. What would it be like to have a little space in my day? How do I feel about letting go of some tasks or projects? Would that be freeing? Would that be scary?

3. "There is only one thing important, to do all from the love that is found in the heart, to do all this with love." In what ways does what I do originate with the love found in my heart? In what ways are there other feelings or needs that motivate me?

The Sharing and Closing Prayer

 *nicodemus*

(John 3:1–10)

The Grace

To break down the walls behind which I hide myself.

The Setting

The Story

The Most Reverend Gabino Zavala, D.D., J.C.L., V.G., was born in Mexico and emigrated to the United States with his family when he was a child. He is an auxiliary bishop for the Archdiocese of Los Angeles and also serves as the California Catholic Conference liaison for detention ministry. He has been rector at St. John's Seminary in Camarillo.

"Rabbi, we know that you have come from God . . . teach us."
    I wanted . . . want . . . still want to meet him.
    I need to make my way to that part of town that I am not familiar with.
    I need to go, to see, to experience. . . . I will be born again . . . by water and the Spirit.
    I am a part of our Institution. . . . I represent this system.
    My world separates me from . . . stories like Naomi's, like David's.
    I am a priest, a canon lawyer, a bishop. My "work" is often so focused on the internal that it engages my whole being. Many times I lose sight of the universal — and find myself far from the persons whose beings I am called to and long to touch.
    I need to go, to see, to experience . . .
    I want, still want to meet him.

My desire to meet the Lord, to know Jesus, has taken me to corners in my faith journey that I never would have darkened, to places and parts of the world otherwise unknown.

I will be born again of water.

I have been asked to celebrate the Liturgy of the Eucharist on Mother's Day at Twin Towers, the women's prison. What can I say? What do I have to say to these women, these mothers? I wish them a happy Mother's Day; they cry. I try to break open the Word. To offer consolation and hope, the reassurance of God's love and mercy, salvation through Jesus' bold and redemptive act, knowledge that the Spirit of the Lord is truly in our midst.

I will be born again of water.

It is my turn to listen to story after story of neglect, abuse, and abandonment. To hear about unfulfilled dreams, hopes, desires, needs. To be reminded of circumstances — life and death, displacement, despair, hunger, the burden of responsibility, caring for others, children, parents, extended family members — that led to their being here, incarcerated. And I weep, water from my eyes falls, for life and lives diminished, torn asunder, wasted and lost. I cry, wail, from a spot deep within. I am a part of a system that is vindictive and punitive, that has not heard the cry of the poor, that can't see the plank in its own eye but magnifies the speck in another's. I am a part of an institution whose body is Christ yet wavers in its love and compassion for those in need.

I see women of strength and beauty, mothers who would lay down their lives for their children. Persons with dignity, who command respect, those talented, unique individuals with unfettered determination and unfathomable potential. Women who have borne the pain of childbirth and the greater pain of separation, whose hope is palpable.

And something sears inside of me. I experience the wrenching pain of reimagining.

The tears — water that admits shame and that sustains conviction — flow. I have met Jesus, the Lord in our midst.

I have been reborn in water.

I will be reborn in the Spirit.

I have been reborn, rebirthed in tears that shout dignity, value and purpose. I have seen spirits undaunted, determined to find *the way,* a way. I have experienced their energy, am touched by their insight, enlightened by their wisdom, their unconventional creativity. The walls of my prisons expand, begin to crumble.

A new passion arises in me, the Spirit wells within me, a spark ignites. I must travel outside the boundaries that define me, the services that hold me at bay, the systems that capture my attention. I have met Jesus, the Lord in our midst.

I have been reborn in the Spirit.

I will never be the same.

— BISHOP GABINO ZAVALA

The Scripture

Among the Pharisees there was a ruler of the Jews named Nicodemus. He came to Jesus at night and said, "Rabbi, we know that you have come from God to teach us, for no one can perform miraculous signs like yours unless God is with him."

Jesus replied, "Truly, I say to you, no one can see the kingdom of God unless he is born again from above."

Nicodemus said, "How can there be rebirth for a grown man? Who could go back to his mother's womb and be born again?" Jesus replied, "Truly, I say to you: Unless one is born again of water and the Spirit, he cannot enter the kingdom of God. What is born of the flesh is flesh, and what is born of the Spirit is spirit. Because of this, don't be surprised when I say: 'You must be born again from above.'

"The wind blows where it pleases and you hear its sound, but you don't know where it comes from or where it is going. It is like that with everyone who is born of the Spirit."

Nicodemus asked again, "How can this be?" And Jesus answered, "You are a teacher in Israel, and you don't know these things!"

The Meditation

> it was a hot evening
> all morning long
> > we had conducted our meeting
> the leaders of israel

were threatened by this one
    called jesus
i knew
walking back to my house
    that i wanted to meet him
talk to him
find out
    why so many of our people
    were listening to him

walking along the crowded street
soon found out
where i could find
where jesus was staying
this was not very difficult
    to discover
they said
all day long
he would receive visits
from the people

i needed
    to wait till the sun set
    till it was dark
i could not go now
    in the daylight
many were saying
that his way
    is very different
    from our legalistic way
made my way
to the part of town
    i was not that familiar with
finally it was dark enough
    there was no moon
i put my hood over my head
as i hurried along

the dirt street
wondered
    if this is how
    i live my whole life
    hiding who i really am
    always wondering
    what others think
    about me
    having to be hidden
    in the dark
to be who
i really am
just knew during
these last years
at the temple
i have not been happy
    there has been an emptiness
    inside
a restlessness
    the self-righteousness
    of my fellow workers
    erased any feeling
of god
that i yearned for

asked someone in front
if she knew
where the master jesus
was staying
    at the end of the street
    a small clay wall
    in front of the house
passed through the entrance
    knocked on the door
the echo from the knock
sounded through the whole house

a young girl answered the door
    why was i so nervous?
i found it hard
to find the right words
    yes i am looking
    for the one they call jesus

she looked at me
    with question marks
    in her eyes

i am sure
i am the first of our institution
    to visit this hidden house

she invited me in
there were all sorts
    of people within
i glanced around the courtyard
i recognized some of the faces
had visited their farms
    to collect the taxes
    necessary to keep alive
    our religion
this money was necessary
    for the treasury
a bent-over face was nearby
i remembered
    he did not have the money
    he was forced off his land
the laws for the poor
    are unjust
    they crush them to death
    there is no mercy
this same young girl
called me to come
to the back of the house

jesus was sitting
talking with a couple
he saw me
finished his conversation
with them
then accompanied me
    outside to the very end
    of the courtyard
    near a fire burning
jesus offered me a seat
    across from him
i could feel strongly
    that he was wondering
    what i was doing
    in his territory
    usually we are his enemies
and here i was asking
    to meet with him
those in the distance
kept an eye
on what
was happening

jesus
my name is nicodemus
    i belong to the sanhedrin
    my family also has for many years
for these months jesus
you have caused discussions
    very heated
in terms of what you are doing
with our people
    they are responding to you
    like they have not done
    for so long
the sanhedrin does not like this

they are afraid
    of what rome is going to think

i was speaking so quickly
was so nervous
    that jesus
    had not said one word
he was just sitting there
listening to what i was saying
i looked at his face
    he looked like he had worked hard
    very tired
    he had dark circles around his eyes
    there was a weariness about him
but these days in jerusalem
it seems everyone is feeling like that
    i was struck by his attentiveness
    in spite of his weariness

nicodemus
thank you for taking the risk
to visit me here
    i know this would not be
    very popular
    with your friends
know you are not used
to this part of town
now i have heard
    what your fellow priests
    think about me
interesting
but you nicodemus
    what do you think?

i was not expecting this question
what do i think?
looked inside myself

i think jesus
    your message
    has much truth
    i have listened to you
    speaking to the crowds
    you are a real teacher
    not like
    our trained religious high priests
what i find in you jesus
    is you see the truth
    in what is right before us
but we don't want to accept it
    the laws of the temple
    the taxes of the romans
are choking to death our people
the sickness the misery
    that is present in our people
makes me sad
jesus
you have something to say
    to this

at that moment
a woman of fifty
came close
to serve us a warm drink

nicodemus
    i would like you
    to meet naomi
she smiled
    stretched out her hand
    very innocently
nicodemus
    i would like you
    to listen for a moment
    to the story of naomi

she sat across
from the fire
flames lighting up
her aged features

ten years ago
i had five children
my husband left me
i could not get work
i had nowhere to turn
my family is from the province
not the city
i was desperate
to feed my children
i stole bread
I was caught
the romans brought me
to their infamous prison
for ten years
i was separated
from my children
i was abused
by the guards in the prison
all for stealing bread

my face changed
my expression turned
grave
i said simply
how is it possible
that this could happen?
such acts
are offenses against god
are totally unfair
i will see
what i can do about it

jesus turned to me
    nicodemus
your world separates you
from stories like naomi's
    if you had all night
    i would walk with you
    around this courtyard
    you could listen
    to one story after the other
    of how
        the poor have been treated
        stepped upon
        caused by the laws
        that crush them

naomi agreed with jesus
    it has never been so hard
    for us
    it is only lately
    with the good news of jesus
    that we are able to be together
    trying to see how to survive
naomi said she had to go
excused herself very gently
    i gave her
    a piece of paper
    how to reach me

nicodemus
unless you are born again
unless you see how the majority
of our country lives
    you will never have life
    you will think that you have life
    but it will be privileged life
    cut off
    from the real life

and god will be far away
from this experience

jesus invited
    david to come over
    this young man
    sat across from the fire
jesus asked him
to speak about the tributes
that had to be paid
to the temple
david explained that his family
had a farm
    but every year
    their taxes were greater
    and greater
his father was killed in an accident
their land was taken over
by the high priests
the money for the sale of the farm
went into the temple's treasury

i realized that this was my treasury
    i represented
    this system

david came here to jerusalem
became immersed in addictions
he did not care about anything
    life was cruel
    was unfair
    his anger was eating him up
    he was hardly ever sober
then one day
he was walking home at noon
he saw in the distance
a crowd gathered

he came closer
he noticed
that there was someone
speaking animatedly
he came closer
he sat down under
the shade of the tree
listened
to what jesus was saying
his message exploded inside of him
he felt at that moment
he did not need to give up
because of the despair
that he had been thrown into
that he could rise above
the darkness
he knew it would not be easy
but it would be possible
that afternoon changed his life
since the time
that he has followed jesus
his life has found meaning
he has been able to forgive
those who did that to his family
he has found peace
for the first time in years
there is something within him
that sings at night
with pure happiness

listening to this young man
i was beginning to understand
the power jesus
had over his followers
his concern
his care was so great

that it was transforming
that he was instilling
    into the people
    that there was a way
    out of the slavery
    the misery
    that they had been living for years
david also excused himself
now there
was only jesus and myself

so nicodemus
    would you like to be born again?
    would you like to join your lot
    with those here this evening?
i felt panic inside
i was used to a standard of living
    so high
i belonged
to such a privileged class
what was jesus asking me?
    to leave all that?

i began to see my life
    differently in that moment
    had never met anyone
like naomi or david
    i was so protected

yes jesus
    i would like to be born again
but i know this is only
a beginning
i need to go
    to see where naomi
    was jailed for ten years
i need to experience

how it is possible
  that such cruel injustice is done
to the most vulnerable of our society
i need to travel
  to the province to see
  how the workers are living
i know i can never
  really begin unless i do all this
this was the moment

yes jesus
  i would like to be born again
i looked into jesus' eyes
even though they were tired
i could tell
  there was a trace
  of joy
  that spread
  across his face
that was manifested
  in the light in his eyes
to be born again
thank you master
  for this lesson
  you have given me tonight

jesus stood up
  accompanied me to the door
i knew
i would never be the same
after
  what i had experienced
  inside this house
knew something powerful had happened
  to be born again

The Anointing and Reflection

1. Do I sometimes feel that I have to hide who I really am? From what do I have to hide and from whom do I have to hide?

2. In what ways am I protected from those whose lives are broken, those who are in pain, those who are alone? In what ways am I connected to those whose lives are broken, those who are in pain, those who are alone?

3. In what ways do I work to build the walls that protect me from others? In what ways am I open to those walls coming down? Do I want to be born again? and again?

The Sharing and Closing Prayer

 well

(John 4:5–26)

The Grace

To be the authentic person that I am at my heart's center, where I also find God.

The Setting

The Story

Cassandra Gonzalez is in prison at Chowchilla Women's Prison in California. She met Mike Kennedy while she was at Central Juvenile Hall in Los Angeles. She is eighteen years old.

I once was the woman at the well. My life was similar to hers. The Lord offered me water that made me thirsty no more, and I felt it in my center. I am no longer numb. I am no longer lonely or live that lie.

Most of my life it seems I've lived a lie — one that I myself don't even understand. I always had an emptiness in my heart. I felt alone for many, many years. I craved death. I was lost in an indescribable, sickening world, a dreamland from which I never awoke. I was tired before I was even born. I was never good enough in the eyes of the "righteous," and I was disgusted with the whole idea of life.

I have six brothers and sisters. While I was growing up I never had a father. I never really knew who he was, although a few of us had an idea. I had a stepfather who passed away from a drug overdose two years ago.

My mother was an alcoholic. But no matter what happened or how drunk she was, she managed to feed us, clothe us, and give us a home. I watched my mom get beat up by my stepfather on several occasions and saw him nod off when he was coming off heroin. I was numb to it all. He was in and out of prison. My mom was sober off and on. After being sober for a while, she couldn't do it any longer. She always asked me for permission to drink. She would say, "Just one drink, I'll just buy one beer. Please, can I? Then that's it." Not knowing better and never learning from past mistakes, I continued to say yes, hoping this time she would mean what she said. I wanted my mom to be happy, and I felt the only way for her to be happy was if she had her alcohol. To this day I wonder if she asked me in the hope of me one day saying no!

Manipulating and deceiving became a big part of my personality. I practiced it so much that I manipulated myself, my mind, and my feelings, which led me to be confused and never know myself. To this day, I still struggle with my past and ways that I am trying to overcome, and a reputation that I am trying to redeem.

Then I surrendered and gave it all to God, and for the first time, I *felt.*

You will never find an answer in the world to satisfy your ways. But the answer lives within and is in your face, knocking on your door.

My grandmother was the well that stored the water because she always had the love of God in her. But I never listened, never opened my eyes to realize it and accept it. Just as Jesus, a Jew, talked to a Samaritan woman when it was forbidden and unusual so my grandmother favored me, the "black sheep," the "bad seed." My grandma had the answers to my questions and the key to my feelings, but I never heard her calling even if she yelled. But my grandmother kept my family together. Without her we would still be lost and numb. Thanks to God, and to God working through her, they saved my life and my family's. No matter what I did, like Jesus she forgave me.

Thank you Jesus and Grandma. I love you!

— CASSANDRA GONZALEZ

The Scripture

Jesus came to a Samaritan town called Sychar, near the land that Jacob had given to his son Joseph. Jacob's well is there. Tired from his journey, Jesus sat down by the well; it was about noon. Now a Samaritan woman came to draw water and Jesus said to her, "Give me a drink." His disciples had just gone into town to buy some food.

The Samaritan woman said to him, "How is it that you, a Jew, ask me, a Samaritan and a woman, for a drink?" (For Jews, in fact, have no dealings with Samaritans.) Jesus replied, "If you only knew the Gift of God! If you knew who it is that asks you for a drink, you yourself would have asked me and I would have given you living water."

The woman answered, "Sir, you have no bucket and this well is deep; where is your living water? Are you greater than our ancestor Jacob, who gave us this well after he drank from it himself, together with his sons and his cattle?"

Jesus said to her, "Whoever drinks of this water will be thirsty again; but whoever drinks of the water that I shall give will never be thirsty; for the water that I shall give will become in him a spring of water welling up to eternal life."

The woman said to him, "Give me this water, that I may never be thirsty and never have to come here to draw water." Jesus said, "Go, call your husband and come back here." The woman answered, "I have no husband." And Jesus replied, "You are right to say: 'I have no husband'; for you have had five husbands and the one you have now is not your husband. What you said is true."

The woman then said to him, "I see you are a prophet; tell me this: Our fathers used to come to this mountain to worship God; but you Jews, do you not claim that Jerusalem is the only place to worship God?"

Jesus said to her, "Believe me, woman, the hour is coming when you shall worship the Father, but that will not be on this mountain or in Jerusalem. You Samaritans worship without knowledge, while we Jews worship with knowledge, for salvation comes from the Jews. But the hour is coming and is even now here, when the true worshipers will worship the Father in spirit and truth; for that is the kind of worship the Father wants. God is spirit and those who worship God must worship in spirit and truth."

The woman said to him, "I know that the Messiah, that is the Christ, is coming; when he comes, he will tell us everything." And Jesus said, "I who am talking to you, I am he."

The Meditation

sitting down
next to jesus
being offered cool water
drinking this water
    water so deep
    that i will never
    have the need
    to drink again
jesus
i sit here
next to you
    against this well
    of our ancestors
jesus
there are always
so many distractions
in my life
now after drinking this water
    you have given me
i feel focused
jesus
my mind is not running
all over the place
feel i can concentrate
    water flowing
    down deeper and deeper
jesus
i came here
there were so many things
on my mind

i was distracted
    by all the responsibilities
    all the messes
    i have gotten
    myself into
jesus
    sitting here
    next to you
    drinking the water
        you offer me
    everything is different
this water
    is flowing
    to my center
speaking
with you
    i see clearly
    how i had taken
    a step
    off the road
but feel
being with you
    that it is possible
    to get back on
    the road
jesus
looking at me
    do you ever
    just let go
    of all your thoughts
        preoccupations
    go inward?
    get to a still place
        where nothing moves
        a silence
        being connected to your center?

jesus
that is what
right now
at this moment
the water
you have given me
 has permitted me
  to calm my mind
  stop the whirlwind of thoughts
  that constantly possess me
jesus
staring out at the cactus
looking up at the blue sky
 drinking this water
 sitting next to you
i think you are
 the one our people
 have been waiting for
in all of life
in all the religious services
i have never
 experienced a depth like this
 jesus there is a contentment
 that sings at my depths
something more is happening
in this time
 with you
i feel different
that i can be the person
 i am supposed to be
 rather than being forced
 to be
  what everyone else
  wants me to be
jesus
i have had five husbands

each one
demanded i change
i could never be
who i am
as a result
i have been unhappy
until i came
to this well
this afternoon
not expecting anything
and i have found
at my depths
a peace
i have not felt
for many years
i realize
being with you jesus
how important
it is in life
to let this water flow
to the center
to stop all the confusion
to feel one greater
at the depths
a presence strong

i never forget that afternoon
it was so strong
i went into town
jesus stayed with us
for a week
after he left
i would wander back
to this spot
in the early morning
i would remember

that experience
    of drinking cool water
letting it flow
    to my center
i have been able to hang on
    to this inner peace

after he left
rumors of his healings
    then being killed
    then his being seen alive
got back to me

sometimes
    even after all these years
    when i come to the well
i am sure
this one is with me again
it only lasts a moment
    but i feel it
    in my very depths
    from where
    i have learned to live
    during these years
this has helped me
    to struggle to be who i am
i no longer let men use me
looking back now
    many years later
to that afternoon
drinking that water
feeling it fall
    down to my center
i think
    it was all about love
something happened to my heart
    i was no longer the same

everyone in the town
said the same
drinking water
reaching my center
changed me
forever
at last
i could be the person
god
desired i become

The Anointing and Reflection

1. Have I ever experienced "a still place where nothing moves, a silence, being connected to your center"? If yes, what brought me to that place? What does it feel like inside me when I am in that place? If no, do I believe that place exists? Do I desire the experience of that place?

2. How might an experience of being connected to my center bear fruit in my life?

3. Am I "the person God desired I become"? What helps me to move toward being that person? What prevents me from becoming that person?

The Sharing and Closing Prayer

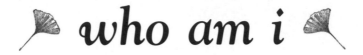

who am i

(Mark 8:27–35)

The Grace

To know Jesus as he truly is and to have the courage to follow him.

The Setting

The Story

Marlon Rivera began studying at Santa Clara University in January 2001 and plans to become a lawyer. He spent four years in Juvenile Hall, California Youth Authority, and in INS detention awaiting deportation before a court ordered his release.

I strongly believe that happiness and sadness go hand in hand. That is, they depend on one another. I turned twenty-one today, but I don't ever recall turning seventeen, eighteen, nineteen, or twenty. When I tell my friends that I feel old they say, "You're crazy!" I never thought that I would be sitting here writing this paper on a computer, much less on the campus of a private university. Earlier today, I walked into class and all my friends smiled at me and whispered, "Happy Birthday!" What beautiful smiles they had for me.

The last birthday I celebrated was my sixteenth birthday. I went to Las Vegas with some friends. What a wild time we had! We had booze, drugs, and women galore. I was gang affiliated, which influenced my story and my perspective. I spent many days in jail after that birthday celebration in Vegas. Some people sent me birthday cards; some

didn't bother. I had nothing to celebrate. My days were always the same. It didn't matter whether it was Monday or Friday, Christmas or Thanksgiving. Neither came after nor before the other, so Christmas came when it came, not in the beginning or at the end of the year. I had no concept of time I didn't care about what I could not control. So I never aged, or I forgot the feeling of what a birthday should feel like. There was nobody with a nice smile to greet you. There were no phone calls. There were no happy wishes from friends. Nobody asked you, "So what are you gonna do?" There was none of that, nobody cared, so why should you? I also built a defense mechanism to keep me from getting hurt: I expected nothing. I never expected to get out of that cell. There was no hope in me for a birthday cake or a smile. That died in me.

Last night I opened a book to a page that read, "Those who have seen the dark are also able to see the light." I live life in a new light. I wake up and go to sleep thinking of how great suffering and joy are, how equally fulfilling they both are. Have you ever died and come back to life? Well, I'd like to think that I have.

I lost in my old life and I refuse to lose in this one. I lived an enclosed life as a teenager. If it had to do with school, it wasn't cool. I was who I was and I can't change that. But that's who I was in the past sense; I am different now. I lost my best friends because of gangs, but I also learned the reality of life because of them and my involvement. I know the "darkness."

Many a time I sat in the dark, looking at the small glimmer of sunlight that barely made it through those dirty rusted windows and how it bounced off the cold cement. It was the only life that came into that place. I looked at that little piece of life and I thought about mine. I was always very popular and liked by the girls, hated by the guys. I thought of my family and where I went wrong, my friends and how I influenced them to mess up their lives. I thought about those things I once had and then lost even before I went to jail. I didn't allow myself to do things like go to the prom, winter ball dances, and the like. I didn't go out with friends outside of my gang, I always waited until a girl made the first move. I would not love because that was too much of a risk. I still remember sitting on that cot in the freezing cold, shivering with nothing but memories to go over until they got old. I remember it vividly.

Sitting in class at Santa Clara as Fr. Paul Fitzgerald taught a course on Catholic theology and spirituality, I noticed two girls passing a note to each other. While I looked at them, my heart felt warm and some laughter and a smile overcame me. I thought about my days in Unit M-N in Juvenile Hall. I was not supposed to get out. Nobody else did. I ask myself, am I dreaming? I can't be in a classroom watching two girls passing notes to each other. This is a memory of high school repeating itself. Am I in high school, Santa Clara University, or in a concrete jail cell?

I told myself for so long that I would never see the light of life. Yet God brings the sun down from space and puts its warmth all around me and so close that the cold cement floor and the dirty window almost cease to exist. The sight of the two free human beings passing a note to each other is a pure luxury. I am grateful.

— MARLON RIVERA

The Scripture

Jesus set out with his disciples for the villages around Caesarea Philippi; and on the way he asked them, "Who do people say I am?" And they told him, "Some say you are John the Baptist; others say you are Elijah or one of the prophets."

Then Jesus asked them, "But you, who do you say I am?" Peter answered, "You are the Messiah." And he ordered them not to tell anyone about him.

Jesus then began to teach them that the Son of Man had to suffer many things and be rejected by the elders, the chief priests, and teachers of the Law. He would be killed and after three days rise again. Jesus said all this quite openly, so that Peter took him aside and began to protest strongly. But Jesus turning around, saw his disciples very close. So he rebuked Peter saying, "Get behind me, Satan! Your thoughts are not from God, but from man."

Then Jesus called the people and his disciples and said, "If you want to follow me, deny yourself, take up your cross and follow me. For if you choose to save your life, you will lose it; and if you lose your life for my sake and for the sake of the Gospel, you will save it."

The Meditation

so much had been happening
every day that i go out
i find that my world
    is stretched
most of the time
    i do not understand
how jesus performs
so many wonders

last night
before i slept
i was worried
    how jesus was acquiring
    so many enemies
    so many complaints
we walked to the lake
it was after breakfast
we were seated around
talking about
    the last week
it was already hot
    we needed the shade
    of the trees
could tell
that jesus was thinking
of something
    he wanted to tell us
we finished breakfast
friends i have been thinking
    who do you think i am?
    who do people say i am?

silence

i know
people are saying all sorts

of things who i am
some say i am
    one of the prophets
but i want to know
    who do you think i am?
    what am i about?

jesus taking the cup
drinking his beverage
i came over
    to where jesus
    was seated
staring out
    into the distance

i came over
sat down
next to jesus
    you are the one
        we have been waiting for
    you are the messiah
jesus
    you have turned
    our world upside down
you have shown us a way
that we can follow
i watched jesus' face
    as i spoke
i could tell
after being with jesus
for so long
    that jesus was pleased
    with what i said

peter
    you have been gifted
    with this understanding

but
i need to tell you all
    being god's anointed
    is going to be costly
i am going to have
    to suffer greatly
to build my abba's reign
    could even cost me my life
cold currents
    spread through the circle
    no one wanted
    to ask anything
    death?
what is jesus talking about?
death?
we are growing in number
we're getting stronger
to be killed?
now wait a minute
peter thought
    i need to talk to jesus
still no one said anything
we were too shocked
first we see
    the importance of naming
    the one we are really following
then he talks
about how
    this will have consequences

silence

slowly everyone
around the breakfast circle
began to leave
    here was my opportunity
jesus seemed heavy

he also seemed preoccupied
concerned
just watching the movements
in the distance
    jesus
        i need to talk
        with you
i know
you have been called
by god
    that you are the one
    we have been waiting for
but what do you mean
that you are going to suffer
    and be put to death?
jesus stood up agitated
    peter don't you see?
    don't you understand?
so many people
    in the villages
    just seem
    to want more and more
        to accumulate
        to be safe
    to do anything
    to avoid suffering
    at all costs
you are thinking peter
like the powerful
you are thinking
like those who are blind
who are only seeking
their own kingdom
riches honor glory
    peter
    i am about something different

i am about
    a new way of seeing
      of acting

this way will make
the powers uncomfortable
they will want
    to destroy me
    can you accept this?
can you also
accept this mystery:
    that we need to give
    our life away
then we will have life
when nothing
    is left
see that house over there
    that elder of the synagogue
    leaving?
all of his life
he has been successful
he has a great reputation
wealth status
is this what you want peter?
that way of thinking
    will never make you happy
    never
peter don't you understand
there is a price
to pay
for building my abba's reign
peter
trust me
my way leads
    to life

The Anointing and Reflection

1. Who do I say that Jesus is? What do I believe he was really about? Who is he in my own life? Who is he for the world?

2. What is my understanding of the price of following Jesus? How have I experienced that price in my own life?

3. "Trust me, my way leads to life." When I read that statement of Jesus how do I feel? What is his way for me? Does it lead to life?

The Sharing and Closing Prayer

rich man

(Mark 10:17–30)

The Grace

To have the faith in Jesus to follow him with complete freedom.

The Setting

The Story

Fr. Greg Boyle, S.J., is the director of Jobs For A Future / Homeboy Industries in Los Angeles, which finds jobs and provides hope for gang members seeking to change their lives. He has worked with gangs and advocated positive solutions to youth crime and violence for over fifteen years.

I send Louie to his first job ever. The employer has assured me that he'll hire whomever I send. Louie is twenty-six years old and has been locked up since he was eighteen. He is stocky and, on first glance, maybe even menacing. God has forgotten to give him a neck, and both arms are alarmingly tattooed. Louie wants this job and longs only that his daughter "feel proud to see me when I walk into the room."

Two weeks after the interview, Louie appears, forlorn, in my office — a jobs referral program. He tells me that he has yet to hear from this prospective employer. Thinking he has been on the job these two weeks, I call the employer. "Was there a problem with the guy I sent you?" Apparently there was. "The guy you sent me kept asking me about the different machines we had. You know, 'What's that machine for?' and things like that. So I figured he was casing the joint. You know, he might come back later with his friends."

I try to console Louie. "We'll have better luck next time." How hard
it is to take seriously what Jesus took seriously. It "costs us" to live the
gospel — to live as though the truth were true.

— GREG BOYLE, S.J.

The Scripture

*Just as Jesus was setting out on his journey again, a man ran up, knelt before
him and asked, "Good Master, what must I do to have eternal life?"*

*Jesus answered, "Why do you call me good? No one is good but God
alone. You know the commandments: Do not kill, do not commit adultery,
do not steal, do not bear false witness, do not cheat, honor your father and
mother." The man replied, "I have obeyed all these commandments since my
childhood."*

*Then Jesus looked steadily at him and loved him and he said, "For you,
one thing is lacking. Go, sell what you have and give the money to the poor,
and you will have riches in heaven. Then come and follow me." On hearing
these words, his face fell and he went away sorrowful for he was a man of
great wealth.*

*Jesus looked around and said to his disciples, "How hard it is for those
who have riches to enter the kingdom of God!" The disciples were shocked
at these words, but Jesus insisted, "Children, how hard it is to enter the
kingdom of God! It is easier for a camel to go through the eye of a needle
than for one who is rich to enter the kingdom of God."*

*They were more astonished than ever and wondered, "Who, then, can be
saved?" Jesus looked steadily at them and said, "For humans it is impossible,
but not for God; all things are possible with God.*

*Peter spoke up and said, "We have given up everything to follow you."
Jesus answered, "Truly, whoever has left house or brothers or sisters, or
father or mother, or children, or lands for my sake and for the Gospel, will
not lose his reward. I say to you: even in the midst of persecution he will
receive a hundred times as many houses, brothers, sisters, mothers, children,
and lands in the present time, and in the world to come he will receive
eternal life."*

The Meditation

            rafael walked
                    by the large storehouses
            he watched
                    as his workers
                            unpacked the imported cloth
            all his life
            rafael enjoyed the luxuries
                    of his class
            as he walked by the center
                    of town
                            all those around the plaza
                            respectfully greeted him
            rafael was restless
                            there was something
                            not right about his life
                            his insides were seeking
                            something someone

            he met his friends
                    outside of the city
            they were going to walk
            to where jesus
                    was preaching

            walking together
            rafael was glad
            to be away from work
            he wanted
                    this afternoon
                    to meet this master
                            whom everyone was talking about
            what was he looking for?
            as rafael walked and talked
            he was mildly distracted
                    thinking about his last deals

in the distance
rafael saw a man
    talking with a group
    he was seated on a rock
    watching the water flowing
seemed like
    he was someone familiar
    had seen him before
soon arriving
rafael approaching the group
    excited
    about finally arriving

jesus standing up
greeting rafael
    my name is jesus
    may i help you?

yes jesus
how do i find
    the answer
    to what i have been
looking for?
    eternal life
i am not satisfied
with my life
    help me
rafael
    could feel a deep presence
    he knelt down
master
what should i do?
all my life
i have been righteous
    have given generously
    to the synagogue
    have not done anything wrong

as rafael talked so quickly
    kneeling in the dust
jesus looked intensely
    at him

rafael
    stand up
    i have something hard
    to say
if you want eternal life
if you want to follow me
    take all your possessions
    sell them
    give the money
    to the poor

there was a silence
a once enthusiastic young man
silent

a thousand thoughts
went around in his head
    in his heart

go sell
    what i have
    and give it to the poor?

rafael
remembering back
    to the cool pool
    outside his villa
    the liquor he enjoyed
    after a lengthy meal
    his large house
    in the middle of the city
    near the plaza
sell those things?

thinking
>   i came here
>   for some advice
>>   and this master
>>   wants to change
>>   my whole life

rafael could feel
the heavy weight
of his numerous possessions
his wealth
>   why would i want to do this?
>   i already am good

rafael chose

the weight
>   from his possessions
>   was too
>>   heavy

i don't want
>   to waste my life
i want to be someone
i want to build up
>   my future
>   to pass this on to my children

jesus
invited sarah
>   standing nearby
>   to come closer
rafael
>   ask this woman
>   what she is now doing
she used to have
so many things
heavy upon her

she wanted
    to be free
she sold everything
sarah now walks with us
she has been
    with us
    for a year
i look at you rafael
i can feel all the weight
    of things you are attached to
rafael started to shake
    i can't let go
    of all this
    these things
    mean too much

jesus saying
    rafael may i ask you
    something?
have any
    of your material possessions
    ever made you happy?
what good does it do you
    to have so much?
let go
let go
    and you will be happy

so many memories of possessions
    passed through his mind
watched jesus
    as rafael said nothing
could see the forming
    of tears
    in jesus' eyes
he
cared for this young man

jesus
    i can't
i have to go now
came here
    to talk
    not change my life
i've worked too hard
to build up my kingdom
i want
to pass it on
    to my children

sarah began
    to talk to her friends
we were like this
we thought
    we were going
    to be so happy
    if we had great wealth
we thought
    our luxuries
    would bring us happiness
but as we have
all said before
    by following jesus
we have never been happier
    in our whole life
before we sold everything
    we just worried
    about all our material things
always preoccupied
not being able to sleep
    always busy
    always distracted
we were miserable
just like rafael

how fortunate we are
to have said
        yes

rafael
walked down the hill
rejecting
    an invitation to find
    real life
    happiness
        that never ends

The Anointing and Reflection

1. Am I searching for something? Am I aware that I am searching or is there a feeling of emptiness that I can't quite describe, or a habit that prevents me from being truly free?

2. What am I attached to? Do I have possessions or habits that actually possess me?

3. Are there ways that I reject Jesus' invitation to real life and happiness? What are those ways and do I want to change them?

The Sharing and Closing Prayer

 widow's son

(Luke 7:11–17)

The Grace

To understand and accept the places of loss and pain in my life.

The Setting

The Story

Martha Lujan, M.S., is a licensed marriage and family therapist and adjunct professor at California State University, Los Angeles. She and her husband, Ruben, were a team with Marriage Encounter for seven years and directed Contemplative Prayer Retreats for ten years.

It's been almost a year now since my mother died after a series of strokes. (Stroke runs in my family. My grandmother — my mother's mom — died from a stroke, and my grandfather had a heart attack.) As my mother died, I was at her side along with my brother, my family, and his family. We stayed with her through her last breath. I told her how much I loved her. The day before her stroke, my mother had left a message on my phone asking forgiveness for the many times she had not been very nice with me, and the next day, before she died, I was able to tell her, with words and feeling that welled up from deep inside of me, that of course I forgave her! How many times had I said to our daughter, "If I ever begin to sound like my mother, please, just shoot me!" But now she's gone. I miss her. I miss my dad. My mother died a year ago next month, and my father died thirty years ago next month! My sister died forty-two years ago, and my other sister, twelve years ago.

They're all gone now, and it's just my brother and me. Orphans. My cousin Joe died seven years ago and my favorite cousin, Frank, died two years ago. My close friend died recently too. Lord, you know how much we enjoyed talking together, working together, being together. He was a true friend. My father-in-law died last month. So many deaths. Lord, they're all leaving, going home, I know, to you. But that doesn't make me feel a whole lot better. I'm still alone. Orphan. It makes me realize that I, too, will be there soon, I hope. I could spend this time feeling sad, feeling sorry for myself, lonely, missing them all.

But this morning as I was driving in to work, I was looking toward the mountains and I noticed a flock of birds flying ahead of me. On the side of the road, sitting on top of a telephone pole was a hawk! I love hawks. Hawks and I have a spiritual connection. I watched that hawk until I passed and looked at the sky, so blue, so beautiful, and the mountains, so incredibly magnificent. I offered my morning prayer and heard the words ringing in my ears and pounding in my heart, "Whatever you ask of me . . . yes!" I thought of my husband of forty-three years who e-mails me poems about how much he loves me — just about every day, sometimes with flowers . . . and I thought of our grown children, and their spouses, and their children, our grandchildren . . . and I thought of Christine, our oldest granddaughter, and her husband, and their daughter, our great-granddaughter! Wow! We're great-grandparents! I'm not old enough for that, am I, Lord? She told me the other day that they're expecting their second baby — two great-grandchildren!

And my husband *still* sends me poems of love and romance and flowers, and hugs me when I get home from working all day listening to the terrible problems and struggles that my clients bring me as their counselor. Lord, you didn't leave me orphaned. You didn't leave me alone. I am surrounded by your promise on our wedding day: "You will see your children, and your children's children." And we are no longer children. We are the elders now. We are the wisdom keepers who pass on the wisdom, knowledge, experience, and power of your love that gives the next generation hope to live each day in the awareness of your love.

Thank you, God, my Father, Brother, Friend, my Lover. I can go on now. I know now that out of sadness comes joy, out of each experience of loss, comes gain, and out of those moments when life seems so full of abandonment and despair, we are not alone. We have hope, we have you.

— MARTHA LUJAN, M.S.

The Scripture

A little later Jesus went to a town called Naim and many of his disciples went with him — a great number of people. As he reached the gate of the town, a dead man was being carried out. He was the only son of his mother and she was a widow; there followed a large crowd of townspeople.

On seeing her, the Lord had pity on her and said, "Don't cry." Then he came up and touched the stretcher and the men who carried it stopped. Jesus then said, "Young man, awake, I tell you." And the dead man got up and began to speak, and Jesus gave him to his mother. A holy fear came over them all and they praised God saying, "A great prophet has appeared among us; God has visited his people." And throughout Judea and the surrounding country, people talked about Jesus' deeds.

The Meditation

the hill was steep
the casket was heavy
with the young life
did not feel the weight
of the box of a young boy
his mother's feet
   were bloodied
   did not matter
   her heart was broken
   by the death
   of her son joshua
   her only son
the accident was sudden
   his body had been twisted
   torn

sarah held him
in her arms
for one last time
before
    he was laid
    in this box
her dress was bloodied
her hands drenched
    she was now alone
she had put such hope
    in this twelve-year-old life
after her husband was killed

her life was brightened
with joshua's presence
    it all ended
    in one minute
    no more boy
playing in the fields

now carrying this box
    so many memories
    flowed through her
the grief ripping at her heart
never could she imagine
what it would be like
    to lose a child
as her feet
walked
in the hot dust
it was like
    she was falling down
    a dark hole
        deeper and deeper
trying to catch her breath
feeling as if
she had fallen down

to lose the one
she had given birth to
had given her milk to
had held in her hands
had taught to walk
now she was walking
without him by her side
the first morning
she woke up
    felt an emptiness
within her
      with the realization
      that joshua
      was not there
sarah was waiting
      to hear his voice
      going to his room
      and no one there
walking
      with this box
      she was only left
      with an ache in the heart
reaching the top
      looking into the distance
seeing a small group
      coming up the hill
      jesus looking at sarah
feeling saddened
by experiencing such grief
      in another
the group carrying the box
stopped
jesus approaching
      embracing sarah
      expressing his sorrow
how difficult to be a parent

to lose your child
jesus
was offering her comfort

at first jesus
could not say one thing

but as jesus
embraced sarah
        the presence of joshua
        was so palpable
she knew
could feel that her son
was alive
        that his presence
        was there
filling her heart
giving her comfort
knowing he was with god

jesus wanted
all those to follow him
down through the ages
to know
        how we never really die
jesus wanted to show
all those present
        how close joshua still was
jesus asked them
        to lower the box
bringing out joshua
jesus kneeling down
        putting his hand
        over joshua's heart
slowly
breathing in new life
sarah knew

that her son
could never really die
remembering
jesus' words
    whoever believes in me
    will live forever
forever
do not fear
live forever
eternal life
do you believe?

this eternal life
giving her comfort

jesus did not want
to see sarah hurt any more

joshua slowly sitting up
    after jesus touched him
life
eternal life
a deep mystery surrounding
a once mourning group
eternal life

The Anointing and Reflection

1. How did I feel as I read this? Were there ways the story touched me?

2. Remembering my own experiences of loss, how do I feel when the loss happens?

3. In that time of loss and the days, months, and years that follow, where do I find the strength to go on? Where do I find my hope, my meaning in life?

The Sharing and Closing Prayer

 see

(Mark 10:46–52)

The Grace

To have my eyes opened so that I may see as Jesus sees.

The Setting

The Story

Tanya Quille, M.D., is a psychiatrist specializing in addiction recovery. She works at the University of Miami Medical School in Miami, Florida.

There's a token homeless person
in my neighborhood.
He's black
and so so skinny,
the whites of his eyes are alternatively
red and dark yellow.
Do you think he's on crack?
Do you think he has AIDS?
He wants to be a victim,
somebody's victim,
anybody's victim
if they can pay
or even if they can't;
it's the only relationship he knows.
Can you spare some change?

I talk to him about treatment,
about the hospital.
My neighbor says,
"I'd much rather they beg for my money
than demand my money."

The skinny, barefooted,
barely clothed human says,
"Yes ma'am, I know"
when I stupidly tell him to get help.
We know each other now.
We nod and smile.
Can you spare some change?

On some days there is humor in his face
and I know he sees the absurdity
of himself and of me.
I won't give him money,
but I buy him food.
When I go into the 7–Eleven
I buy him a tuna sandwich.
I hand it to him
and he looks up at me
and says, in his thin so thin voice,
I wanted a Coke.

He says his name is Wilston.

I saw Wilston again last week. I had gone to my old neighborhood. It was night and I was with a friend. Just as we were about to get into my friend's brand new silver Saab convertible, I saw Wilston sitting on the curb. It had been at least seven years since I had seen him. At first I wasn't sure it was him. I thought, no, it can't be him still alive. But it was, and I was really happy to see him, like an old friend. I said, "Wilston?" And he turned his head and said, "Yees." My friend looked at Wilston and was immediately uncomfortable that I was talking to this person. I walked over to Wilston, and he recognized me too. He said, "I haven't seen you in a long time." I said, "I know, I moved. How are you?" And in his thin voice he said, "Oookaay." Still, I asked him, "Did you ever go to treatment?" He said, "I have an appointment this Thursday." I guess I looked hopeful and approving and he smiled at his success of having said the right thing. I said, "I hope you go, please go. It's good to see you, Wilston. Bye." He said, "It's good to see you too." He didn't ask me for anything, and I didn't give him anything. I didn't have any cash on me. And I got in the car with my uncomfortable friend and we drove away leaving Wilston on the same curb where I last saw him over seven years ago.

I think that I should have done more for Wilston, then and now. I don't think he is homeless, because although he is always barefooted, his clothes are clean and he never smells. So I think he must have a family that allows him to come home to bathe and wash his clothes and sometimes sleep. I should have gotten more involved. I should have asked him where his people are, who they are, where they live, and maybe gone to see them to see if there is anything that I can do to help Wilston in a larger way. I think I owe him that. But my life moves so fast and Wilston is just part of the landscape.

— TANYA QUILLE, M.D.

The Scripture

They came to Jericho. As Jesus was leaving Jericho with his disciples and a large crowd, a blind beggar, Bartimaeus, the son of Timaeus, was sitting by the roadside. On hearing that it was Jesus of Nazareth passing by, he began to call out, "Son of David, Jesus, have mercy on me!" Many people scolded him and told him to keep quiet, but he shouted all the louder, "Son of David, have mercy on me!"

Jesus stopped and said, "Call him." So they called the blind man saying, "Take heart. Get up, he is calling you." He immediately threw aside his cloak, jumped up and went to Jesus.

Then Jesus asked him, "What do you want me to do for you?" The blind man said, "Master, let me see again!" And Jesus said to him, "Go your way, your faith has made you well." And immediately he could see, and he followed Jesus along the road.

The Meditation

> the red building
>> where i lived
>> burnt with the strength
>> of the sun

> eighteen steps climbing down
> from my house
> to the street below
> living alone
> everyday as i climbed down
>> an elderly voice
>> yelling out
> bartimaeus blind one
> remember
>> you have eighteen steps
>> to climb down
>> from your red house
> be careful

> and every day
> as she said this
> i desired so deeply within
> to be able to see
> what a red brick building
>> looks like

all my life
having lived in darkness
now being twenty-one
and alone
having to beg
    as an outcast

bringing myself
    to the bottom
    of the stairs
finding the street
    this early morning

on one level
i didn't want to have
    to wander out again
    to beg

all along the street
people greeting me
stumbling
    with my traveling bag
    with my begging bowl
how many years
would i have to live like this?
i want to see
arriving at my place
    it was already hot
being greeted
by the vendors
veronica handing me
    some food

finishing the fruit
hearing
    in the distance
    a noisy crowd approaching
my sense of hearing

was acute
asking veronica
    what was happening
    what could she see
she yelled back
that it
was this journeying preacher
with a large group of followers
something burnt inside

jesus
is finally passing by
    while i am here

didn't hesitate for a moment
jesus i yelled
    i'm over here
    i need your help
i could hear
some vendors coming closer

bartimaeus
    be quiet
    it is jesus
    who is coming
    don't bother him
    be quiet

jesus
stopped nearby
    my voice
    entered into him
    the pain the suffering
    in my voice moved him

jesus
    was in the middle
    of the street

asking peter
    if he knew
    where that voice
    came from
as jesus was saying this
once again
the air was shaken
i yelled
    jesus
    help me
    i need you

jesus
    asking peter
    if he could find
    that person
peter approaching me
helping me come close
to jesus

i knew
i was now
in front of him
jesus
    putting his hand
    on my shoulder
my name is jesus
    i heard your cry
    what is your name?

jesus
    my name is bartimaeus
    can you help me?
all my life
i have been blind
one day
i would like

to leave my house
    my red brick building
i would like to see
what red looks like
i stumble around
in darkness all day
i would like to see

jesus
    putting his hand
    on my head
his strong hand
bore down on my head
bright light flowing
within
    jesus
    i would like to see
he then placed
his hands against my eyes
feeling heat pressure
    jesus
    i want to see
feeling deep emotions
having suffered for so long

bartimaeus
i pray for you
    abba one greater
    let your light flow
    into my brother's darkness
    it is hard to see
    even when we think
        we see

let him
    see with his eyes
    with his heart

so he can see
what this life
is about
to see how to be happy
not how the blind leaders
tell us

may he see
that in being at the bottom
there also is life
to see
that climbing down
the steps
also leads to life

bartimaeus
be healed

i opened my eyes
i looked
into the face
of jesus
i looked into his eyes
he was smiling

stunned
shaken
slowly walking back
along the same street
where i journeyed
every day
climbing up the stairs
with jesus
reaching
where i had lived
for so many years
in darkness
seeing my red brick building

jesus saying
> now bartimaeus
> let us walk down
> these stairs
> don't forget
> that now
>> that you can see
>> with your eyes
> don't forget
> to walk down
> these eighteen steps
> to now help
> the widows the diseased
> at the bottom
>> of the stairs
> may you always
>> also see
>> where god
>> especially dwells below

The Anointing and Reflection

1. Do I have the courage that Bartimaeus showed in calling out to Jesus for help? Do I believe that Jesus will listen?

2. Are there limitations or disabilities in my own life that I would like to ask Jesus to heal?

3. Are there gifts that I have that I do not share with "the widows, the diseased at the bottom of the stairs?"

4. How can I learn to see more with my heart?

The Sharing and Closing Prayer

widow

(Mark 12:38–44)

The Grace

To be able to offer to Jesus and others all that I have.

The Setting

The Story

Mark Raper, S.J., an Australian Jesuit, served in Rome as the international director of the Jesuit Refugee Service from 1990 to 2000. In the 1980s he lived in Bangkok, Thailand, as regional director for JRS activities in Asia and the Pacific.

Gabriel, a six-foot-six Dinka, had arrived in Thailand after a journey that rivaled Marco Polo's. Traveling by foot to escape the fighting that had begun in 1983 in his home in southern Sudan, he had crossed into Egypt and planned to go on to Iran to study, but instead he was drafted to be a porter in the Iran-Iraq war. Escaping, he failed to get passage westward to Europe and then, heading east toward Australia, was stopped in Singapore and diverted to Thailand. There I found him, culturally disoriented, alone, and desperate. He visited frequently, and with an officer from the United Nations High Commissioner for Refugees (UNHCR), we searched everywhere for a country to take him. Australia, New Zealand, the United States, Canada, Sweden, none would even interview him. Finally he was offered three choices: Kenya, Liberia, or a trip home to the Sudan. In desperation he accepted Liberia

and departed around 1987 or '88. Several times he wrote to me, his words dictated to a Scottish Salesian priest.

A few years later I was in my new position in Rome. Deeply moved by the suffering of the Liberian people, I went in 1991 to war-ravaged Monrovia to see what could be done. While there I hunted for Gabriel. Visiting the Salesians, I asked if they had known him. Sure enough, they pointed me to a Scot, the one who had written Gabriel's letters. He told me how Gabriel had died, mistaken for a Mandingo, waving his long arms and showing his refugee card, trying to explain to a drugged, overarmed Krahn follower of Charles Taylor that he was "under the protection" of the United Nations. I wept for Gabriel and the many victims of that senseless, never-ending war.

— MARK RAPER, S.J.

The Scripture

As he was teaching, he also said to them, "Beware of those teachers of the Law who enjoy walking around in long robes and being greeted in the marketplace, and who like to occupy reserved seats in the synagogues and the first places at feasts. They even devour the widow's and the orphan's goods while making a show of long prayers. How severe a sentence they will receive!"

Jesus sat down opposite the Temple treasury and watched the people dropping money into the treasury box; and many rich people put in large offerings. But a poor widow also came and dropped in two small coins.

Then Jesus called his disciples and said to them, "Truly I say to you, this poor widow put in more than all those who gave offerings. For all of them gave from their plenty, but she gave from her poverty and put in everything she had, her very living."

The Meditation

> it seemed that everyone
>> was entering the temple
>> at the same time
> the meeting was over
> the pharisees filed past us

we sat with jesus
along the benches
we could see
from one side of the large pillars
where the treasury box was
the sunlight of the afternoon
was falling down on the benches
the noise from the patio
was strong
there was a long line
of those approaching the box

i saw ezekiel
one of the most respectable
of all the pharisees
he had on his best robes
gold trim
white flowing material

jesus turned to me
and said look at ezekiel
what he has in his hands
ezekiel holding a large canvas bag
full of coins
ezekiel approaching the box
everyone their eyes on him
he offers up a prayer
as an elder
god
i come here everyday
i have brought this gift
in thanksgiving
he then puts the bag
of coins
into the box
it clangs
it falls

the noise vibrates
off the walls
i look at jesus
    his hands are gripped hard

jesus turns to me
you know
    ezekiel has the largest home
    in the plaza
his wife has desired
a new villa every year
they spend more money
on wine in one night
than he just put
into the treasury box
look at how impressed
everyone is
    with his hypocritical generosity
it is blood money
the taxes from the poor
is what finances him
    this system is an offense
    against god

jesus looking around the temple
reflecting on the one
    who made all this world
the feeling of one greater
seeing the long line
    of people
    waiting
    to put in money
seeing the pharisees
    holding their bags of coins
looking at the poor
    from so many faraway provinces
jesus was feeling

so many things
as he gazed
upon this clanging of coins
he wanted to close his ears
nothing seemed to make sense
at that moment
an anger rose in his heart
realizing
what the temple had become
to really depend on his abba
how is ezekiel
doing this
by putting in hardly anything
of what he owns?
as these feelings
flowed through jesus
he glanced and saw susanna
she was near the box
she hobbled
from being bent over
she had spoken with us earlier
she had come here
from a small town
near capernaum
she did not have a place
to stay
susanna was planning to work
to see if she could eat
she did not know
how she would return
to her town
praying as she made her way
god
i do not know
what i will do
if i put this coin

in the treasury box
it is all i have
god
i trust you
that you hold me
in your hands
god
sometimes it seems my life
has been so hard
but you have given
me so much
all my family is dead
i am alone
but i am still alive
i can still serve food
to gain enough to survive
i am deeply grateful
and i love you
tears started to fall
warmly down her face
she picked up her arm
and put in the coin

the pharisees' faces were hardened
this was not much good
for their luxurious living
the coin fell
deeper and deeper
into the treasury box
the temple shook
a subtle change began
to take place
inside the temple
jesus smiled
content that susanna loved
so much

she could give everything
to god
        everything
jesus went over to her
inviting her to eat
with them
now susanna smiled
realizing
        it is only when
        we give everything away
        that we receive all

The Anointing and Reflection

1. What do I hold on to? What do I keep in reserve, just in case? What is my own relationship with money?

2. What might "giving everything away" look like in my life?

3. Have I ever "given everything away" in an act of trust? What was that like? If not, how do I imagine that it might feel? In what small ways might I "give everything away?"

The Sharing and Closing Prayer

temple

(John 2:13–25)

The Grace

To have the wisdom and strength to stand against injustice.

The Setting

The Story

Juan Vargas is the assistant majority leader of the California State Assembly, representing the Seventy-Ninth District (near San Diego). Juan spent a number of years as a Jesuit before graduating from Harvard Law School and practicing law. In 1993 he was elected to the San Diego City Council and in 2001 assumed his current role as a state legislator.

We had just passed the state budget for the upcoming fiscal year, and all I could do was sit numbly at my desk. After fighting hard for three straight days, we were able to save meager funding for foster care, low-performing schools, health clinics, and low-income housing. But to achieve this small victory, we were forced to give millions of dollars in tax benefits to millionaire farmers who didn't need the money. You see, under this system, the only way to save these programs for the poor is to capitulate to the powerful and their supporters in the legislature — so we did.

Yet these powerful people didn't capitulate to their workers. I thought of all the poor *campesinos* arriving early the next morning for work, grinding their bodies into the soil, knowing there was no break for them — only for the wealthy man in the big ranch house. I also thought

162

of the *campesino*'s daughter who emerged from her family's poverty and struggled first to learn English in a crummy rural school, and through her hard work finished at the top of her class — only to learn that she can't go to college because of where she was born. We tried hard, but there was no break for her — only for the wealthy man who treated her family so shabbily.

I couldn't help but think how it was the same old story: the rich using the system to take advantage of the poor and the powerless.

— JUAN VARGAS

The Scripture

As the Passover of the Jews was at hand, Jesus went up to Jerusalem. In the Temple court he found merchants selling oxen, sheep and doves, and money-changers seated at their tables. Making a whip of cords, he drove them all out of the Temple court, together with the oxen and sheep. He knocked over the tables of the money-changers, scattering the coins, and ordered the people selling doves, "Take all this away and stop turning my Father's house into a marketplace!"

His disciples recalled the words of Scripture: "Zeal for your House devours me as a fire."

The Jews then questioned Jesus, "Where are the miraculous signs which give you the right to do this?" And Jesus said, "Destroy this temple and in three days I will raise it up." The Jews then replied, "The building of this temple has already taken forty-six years, and you will raise it up in three days?"

Actually, Jesus was referring to the temple of his body. Only when he had risen from the dead did his disciples remember these words; then they believed both the Scripture and the words Jesus had spoken.

Jesus stayed in Jerusalem during the Passover Festival and many believed in his Name when they saw the miraculous signs he performed. But Jesus did not trust himself to them, because he knew all of them. He had no need of evidence about anyone for he himself knew what there was in each one.

The Meditation

the doves that were to be sold
to offer sacrifice to god
were bound with cord
their sharp feet
stumbled upon the rope
    wrapped around them
    many times the thin rope
    strangled the life
    out of the doves
for the seller of sacrifice
    a lifeless dove
        was worthless

watching jesus
stare
at the dead dove
jesus breathed hard
let out a sigh
    he had made many friends
    with the people
    who had just arrived
    in the temple
last night
    as we walked above
    the city
and listened to the stories
of so many who
had just arrived from the provinces
they were dying of hunger
they were being taxed so greatly
they were being stepped upon
    by the landowners
many of the children
had not made it back
it had been a heavy year

in terms of hunger
for the young
not having the nourishment
to make it back
for another year's sacrifice
and somehow they did not think
it could get worse
everything about their lives was hard
but last night
around the fires
there was a sense of community
a sense that it was worth it
that one day
things will be better
unbelievable
how they find the strength
to continue
jesus now looking at this dove
strangled by the long rope
around and around its neck
i knew what jesus
was thinking
after listening to so many stories
last night
this is what
is happening to the people
the system of taxing
them for the hard work
robbing them
of the chance of survival
and any deviation
meant imminent death
i could feel the anger
coming from jesus
how is it possible
that we have this cord

around the neck
of the people
in this country?
  why?
  what are we going to do
  about this choking cord?
we need to work for a world
where cords do not choke
the poor of this country to death
    we need to work for a country
    that gives a chance
    for its young to go forward

but jesus was sad
a cumulative sense
of how the temple
was choking the life
out of its people
even though
its religious leaders
constantly talk about
how all this
is pleasing god
    this system needs to change
not just move
    one tax collector's table
not just charge farmers
less tax
    but a system
    where a few receive so much
    while the majority
    have to endure
        such deprivation
        and abuse
this is not the will
of the one who made

this whole universe
this one is so much greater

the old the young
of this country
are taken away
by the romans
and never seen again
whenever there is any type of challenge
to the system of the religious elite
        that is all-controlling

the coins
piled so high
on the tables
symbol of such luxury
while
the empty bags of the poor
from the provinces are a sharp contrast
to the large piles of coins

there were tears in jesus' eyes
as he looked
at this dove's lifeless body
symbol of the poor
        feeling such sadness such pain
        having to see such death
        with those whom
        he cared about so much
        as if god also
in this ornate building
        was crying
        was reacting
        against such injustices
        done to his people
even done in his name
this was too much

jesus
invited me
to come over
we took the ends of the table
turned it over
        the coins ran along the floor
        of the patio
clanging
but not as loud as the cries
of the mothers who had to visit
their sons
        after they had been imprisoned
        and tortured by the romans
not as loud
as the old
who worked long hard hours
and then had to give the profits
for the taxes demanded of them
        each year more and more
to satisfy
the insatiable greed
of the powerful
the coins spilled out
of the doors

at first no one moved
all stared at jesus
        as he let out a cry of anger
that he had been carrying
within for so long

no abba
you do not desire
this system that kills
you desire
systems that give life
provide opportunities

not death
    the poor looked hard at jesus
then they also picked up
the ends of the tables
    they turned them over
they did not bother
to pick up the coins
rather the rope
that was around their necks
    was loosened
as they overturned
the tables
there was a realization
in the patio
that perhaps with this effort
they too would not
find themselves lifeless
the next year
with cords strangling them
that with this gesture
they could once again
    feed their children
with this gesture
they could once again
have youth in their homes
    to help
    work the fields
rather than in the inner chambers
of the jails of the romans
a sound of hope
    filled that patio
as the coins rolled out
into the entrance of the temple

no one ever
forgot that moment

old men
>returned to their families
>and talked to their sons
about this one
who was angry enough
at the system
to challenge the idols
of the powerful
>jesus put his faith
>in god
and how they were too many
>too angry
>for any of the temple guards
>to do anything
>about the overturning of the tables
and now when the youth
rehear this story
this gives them
>hope
>that god
>does not want us
>to be choked to death
>like that helpless dove
he wants us to have dreams
to fulfill desires
to walk toward life
not to be choked to death
by endless coils of rope
>god wants to overturn
>systems that choke
>the people
glad there
was this one
who showed
us how god too
>feels the pain of the people

that god's heart
also is filled
with sadness
with anger
when systems are created
that choke people
to death
how important
to remember this event
how much god
desires us to be free
from systems of death

The Anointing and Reflection

1. What is my response to Jesus' anger? How do I feel? What do I think?

2. Are there systems around me that choke the poor, that kill instead of support life? What are those systems and do I play any part in them?

3. Are there ways that I can overturn the tables?

The Sharing and Closing Prayer

feet

(John 13:1–15)

The Grace

To be open to Jesus' intimate love for me and to respond to his call to serve others.

The Setting

The Story

Mario Fuentes was a refugee from El Salvador. He came to the United States in the 1980s after being forced to flee from his country because of his work for justice and reform. He now works at Dolores Mission Church in Los Angeles with base communities and community organizing.

Damian Muñiz graduated from Dolores Mission School in 1999 and attended Salesian High School in Los Angeles.

We first visited sixteen-year-old Damian at Children's Hospital on April 12, 2001. There were twelve of us from the small base communities, and we sat with Damian for a long time, praying for a healing of his leukemia. A few months later, Damian's condition continued to deteriorate. We were told by the doctors that, in order to live, Damian would need great quantities of blood and platelets.

We had the funeral liturgy for Damian last night, September 24, only five months after he had been diagnosed. Dolores Mission Church was filled with his classmates from the parish grammar school and Salesian High School. We are accustomed to having funerals for youth in our church who have been killed by gang violence, but last night was

different. Damian had died the victim of a disease we were all helpless to stop. At the end of the funeral liturgy, Mr. Cortez, Damian's
eighth-grade teacher, tearfully told the congregation how the staff in
the hospital commented on the strength and depth of love of the
community from the church. They said, "We never have seen such
generosity and compassion. No youth here has ever received such large
donations of blood."

The Sunday before Damian died, the same group that visited him
in April prayed around his hospital bed for the last time. Damian was
in pain, his broken body struggled to live with the aid of a breathing
machine. We prayed in a circle and anointed him together, each person
praying over him and offering a blessing.

A few days later, a nurse informed his mother, Lola, that Damian's
liver was failing and death was imminent. Lola placed her head right
beside his ear and said, "*Te amo, mijo. Voy a estar contigo.*" ["I love you,
my son. I will be with you."]. A few tears fell from his nearly closed
eyes, and he died with his mother at his side, holding his hand.

The love of the community was set into motion after Damian died.
The youth from the parish had a food sale and a car wash to help pay
for the funeral expenses. Our base communities had numerous food
sales, for which people stayed up well into the late hours making the
preparations. Past differences were put aside, and a sense of being a
community of service was palpable.

At the cemetery, one of Damian's classmates said, "I have never
thought much about dying till now. I was afraid to visit Damian in the
hospital when he became so weak. But what has moved me is how this
community can celebrate, with love, Damian's life by helping so much.
When I die I hope something like this happens around my family. I
have seen real love."

The Scripture

*It was before the feast of the Passover. Jesus realized that his hour had come
to pass from this world to the Father, and as he had loved those who were
his own in the world, he would love them with perfect love.*

They were at supper; the devil had already put into the mind of Judas, son of Simon Iscariot, to betray him, but Jesus knew that the Father had entrusted all things to him, and as he had come from God, he was going to God. So he got up from table, removed his garment and taking a towel, wrapped it around his waist. Then he poured water into a basin and began to wash the disciples' feet and to wipe them with the towel he was wearing.

When he came to Simon Peter, Simon said to him, "Why, Lord, you want to wash my feet!" Jesus said, "What I am doing you cannot understand now, but afterward you will understand it." Peter replied, "You shall never wash my feet."

Jesus answered him, "If I do not wash you, you can have no part with me." Then Simon Peter said, "Lord, wash not only my feet, but also my hands and my head!"

Jesus replied, "Whoever has taken a bath does not need to wash (except the feet), for he is clean all over. You are clean, though not all of you." Jesus knew who was to betray him; because of this he said, "Not all of you are clean."

When Jesus had finished washing their feet, he put on his garment again, went back to the table and said to them, "Do you understand what I have done to you? You call me Master and Lord, and you are right, for so I am. If I, then, your Lord and Master, have washed your feet, you also must wash one another's feet. I have just given you an example that as I have done, you also may do."

The Meditation

the candles were lighting the room
jesus going
over by the door
    taking from the hook
    a large tan towel
taking off his outer garment
picking up the water basin
the water was warm
the towel
    what was jesus doing?
    why is he doing this?

jesus coming to where
    i was
kneeling down
    in front of me
i was feeling uncomfortable

jesus
what are you doing?
jesus
    taking my feet
    placing them
    in the warm water

peter
when we first met
remember when
we would have such long days?
tonight
your lord and master
will give you an example
    as a friend
i am inviting you
    to do the same
    to wash
    others' feet

jesus taking my feet
into his hands
peter i would like
you to be my friend forever
    i would like
    you not to let
others be treated as inferior
do not try to be number one
rather try
to wash the other's
feet

feeling jesus' hand
against my feet
thinking
of all the faces of the sick
    outside my house
    waiting to be cured
thinking of how i said i would try
    to be more focused
    more concentrated
    on what i am supposed
    to be doing
but just looking
at the sea of faces
waiting for jesus
waiting for him
    to say something
waiting for him to give them hope
feeling jesus' hands
pouring the warm water
against my feet
gripping them hard
feeling this bond
knowing how it is so important
    to wash other people's feet
with the most fragrant oil
anointing my feet
thinking
of all the times
during these months with jesus
that i have helped him
anoint the sick
sometimes i was tired
thought i would die
from being so exhausted
and now here jesus
was doing to me

what i had done to others
did not want this moment
        ever to end
feel the oil
enter deeper and deeper
        into places
        where i had been weak
        during these last months
did not want to move from this place
looking down into jesus' eyes
they were filled with love

he took my feet
into his hands
thanking me
for all the times
i had helped him
letting me know how much
he appreciated
what i had done
how happy
he was
        for working together
        for being about the work
            of one greater
with my feet
in his hands
feeling his love
his gratitude
feeling
these bonds of friendship
to be servant
to minister
to be ministered to
glad i had let jesus
wash my feet

i felt close to jesus
my heart was touched
with this show of his love

The Anointing and Reflection

1. Can I let Jesus wash my feet, "enter deeper and deeper into places where I have been weak"? Has anyone been Jesus for me in that way? How did I feel?

2. Whose feet have I washed? Who have I touched in the places where they have been weak? How do I feel when I wash others' feet?

3. Do I believe that Jesus appreciates my work?

The Sharing and Closing Prayer

 *spirit*

(Acts 2:1–4)

The Grace

To invite the Holy Spirit deeply into my life and to allow the Spirit to guide me.

The Setting

The Story

Mary Ellen Burton-Christie is a spiritual director. She lives in Los Angeles with her husband, Doug, and their nine-year-old daughter, Julia.

The doctors have just told us that my father has only a few hours to live. When we tell him, his face crumples as he tries to communicate, in the only way he can, his sadness and disappointment at hearing the news. For the last fourteen days he has been lying in Room 7 of the intensive care unit of Community Hospital. A machine has been breathing for him, therapists have been moving his arms and legs for him, and we have been struggling to understand what he wants by asking questions that can be answered by a nod or shake of his head. And now things have taken a turn for the worse, and he is really dying. We stand around his bed — my mother, brother, sisters, and cousins. We cry and pray with him and tell him we love him. And we watch the monitor that soon becomes the only way that we know he is still living.

The story that brought us to that room lives in each of us. It is a

story of great pain and great hope. My father suffered from multiple sclerosis (MS) for twenty years, and it changed him and each of us.

One day my father was walking down a city street. He stubbed both his feet on a piece of concrete jutting out of the sidewalk and fell flat on the ground. The fall triggered his first attack of MS. The immediate symptoms were pain in his legs and feet, and a temporary loss of vision in one eye. (Over the years the symptoms became more severe — he could no longer walk and speech became difficult.) Suddenly everything changed. Daddy, who I thought could always do anything and who seemed to have had a plan for our lives, was no longer in control. A very mysterious illness now made his life painful and very uncertain. I saw his frustration and fear, and I became frightened and angry. I could not understand how God could let this happen to my daddy. So I turned to God and asked God to take the MS away. My father and my whole family turned to God to pray for healing.

Healing happened, but it was nothing like we had hoped for or expected. Soon after Daddy's fall we started to go, almost nightly, to a healing service at St. Patrick's Church on the outskirts of Boston. Soon we came to know others who frequented the healing services: "Necco-wafer Mary" (as we called her), who rode the bus each night after working all day at the candy factory, became a favorite of ours. And we always looked forward to seeing Joe, the policeman with the beautiful deep brown eyes. They and so many others greeted us with great warmth and compassion. Soon we learned that Mary worked at her job each day with pain in her legs, and Joe's beautiful eyes saw less and less each day.

Yet there was something else going on. The nightly presence of these people expressed a hope that seemed unfounded. Few of them were actually being healed of their physical illnesses. But they testified compellingly to how their lives were being transformed by the powerful indwelling of the Holy Spirit. Sometimes that experience took the form of speaking in tongues, sometimes they "rested" in the Spirit, sometimes it was the experience of deep peace and a strong connection with others in prayer and friendship. At first it was hard for me not to be cynical about all of this. I wondered whether they were just in denial about their pain and their anger with God for not healing them.

Then I began to see a shift in my father. I saw him — in the midst of great pain, his walking became increasingly difficult — beginning to open to a love that seemed bigger than anything he had ever known before. Instead of asking, "How can God, my loving Father, let this happen to me?" as he had so often toward the beginning of his illness, he began to speak of his MS as a gift! His daily struggle with his pain and disability seemed to have brought him to a deeper realization of his need for God. I watched, astonished, as my father relinquished control of his life to God, as he opened his heart to let God love him, to let God come closer to him.

And now, after twenty years of struggling and pain and joy and a deepening of the experience of God's love, here we are on the day that Daddy will die. It is terrible, my pain is more than I think I can bear. Seeing the pain of my mother and my brother and sisters is maybe even worse.

At that moment, a doctor who has been part of the team that treated Daddy walks in. We thank him for all that he has done. He says, "What we need now is a miracle." We all looked around at each other. As we stand there literally watching the life blood flow out of Daddy, watching the line on the monitor get flatter and flatter, my sister Jane with eyes red from days without sleep and tears flowing down her cheeks says, "I think we've had our miracle." She speaks for all of us. The gift of my father's life, the gift of MS, and — most of all — the gift of the Holy Spirit entering all of our lives in a very powerful way are miracles that have brought us joy and peace, even in the midst of our pain and loss.

— MARY ELLEN BURTON-CHRISTIE

The Scripture

When the day of Pentecost came, they were all together in one place. Suddenly a sound like the blowing of a violent wind came from heaven and filled the whole house where they were sitting. They saw what seemed to be tongues of fire that separated and came to rest on each of them. All of them were filled with the Holy Spirit and began to speak in other tongues as the Spirit enabled them.

The Meditation

returning to the place
    where i began
    returning
yesterday arriving
    at this upper room
two roman soldiers
caught sight of me
    ran upstairs
    as quickly as possible
    fear paralyzing me
all i could think of
    were the scenes
    of jesus tortured
    by soldiers of the empire
arriving here
everyone stopping
asking what had happened
    here i was
        the leader
    the one
    who was supposed
    to be strong
i was trembling
paralyzed by fear
we sat for hours
speaking about
    what was going to happen
the project of jesus
    each day seemed to fade
    in the background

the women seemed
    so much stronger
fear had not taken over
we prayed last night

the women telling us
    it was time
    was time
    to begin to speak
    about jesus
    to begin this project
here i was still terrified
    of being seized
    by the military
looked deep within myself
asking myself
how was i going to be free?
we needed to follow
    the example of the women

this morning we gathered
    to remember the master
we would break bread together
    as we sat
    in the quietest hours
      of the morning
    a stillness filled our room
reading the Scriptures
waiting
    as the watchman
    waits for the dawn
sometimes i have not wanted
    to get out of bed
paralyzed by fear
paralyzed by past days

waiting

outside in the distance
    bells ringing
    sounding subtly
felt jesus' presence

his spirit was here
i yelled out jesus
jesus
something was happening
his spirit
his strength
his vision
    began to come alive
    within
i could feel
    when he cured the leper
could feel
    when he spoke to the multitudes
could feel
    when he walked
    with us

i wanted to touch him
to be with him
    like we had been
    at the shore
    of the lake of galilee
but what we were experiencing
was different
stronger
he was present
i know he had told us
    how he would send
    the spirit
the spirit

    could not think
    could not move
flowing within fire
burning strong
it was at the moment
it was like

huge boulders
being blown apart
opening up
new space
breaking open
dark deep fear
   slipping through walls
my whole body
was trembling
but the difference
   from last night
i was not shaking from fear
but shaking from the power
   of jesus' spirit
   strong
burning strength
entering deep
slowly being healed
   from paralysis
looking around
everything seemed different
   knew i was different
   knew it was time
time to begin
to begin god's project
that jesus was present
   with us
his strength
his spirit
   had taken over the space
   of fear within
his spirit had driven out fear

finding strength within
leaving the upper room
but more importantly

forever leaving behind
fear that paralyzes
that has not permitted me
    to act
    to speak
    to the great numbers
        from so many countries
        gathered in the plaza
looking around
    at the sea of faces
i was no longer paralyzed
by fear
rather i began
    to speak
    telling those before me
    about jesus
        who was the one
        we had been waiting for
        to save us
        save us from the darkness
        surrounding us
but our religious leaders
    could not stand
    this truth
they needed to destroy jesus
but his abba
    raised him up
    and he is alive
i could feel power
strength
felt jesus' spirit
    empowering me
could tell
those in the crowd
    were being moved
    by words flowing out

knew it was this power
that we had been waiting for
so this is what
it is to be filled
with jesus' spirit

all of us
this morning had been changed
each of us
now spoke with feeling
    with conviction
i watched as mary
    one of our group
bent down and touched a leper
with sores oozing
jesus' spirit was so strong
that mary embraced this one
who for years
    had been marginated
    from his family
jesus' spirit was working
    so strongly
that this leper
    was healed instantly
joy spread over his face
my heart was so moved
by spirit overpowering
    that i began to speak clearly
    of my experience
    of knowing jesus
burning feeling within
    that the many
        standing before me
would also know this one
spirit strong burning within
flowing out

The Anointing and Reflection

1. How have I experienced the Holy Spirit in my life? Can I remember a moment of being moved by the Spirit to "speak clearly of my experience of Jesus"? A moment in which fear was transformed?

2. Can I invite the Spirit into my life? What might that mean? How might that change my life?

3. Can others see the life of the Spirit in me? In what ways do I allow the Spirit to live through me? In what ways do I prevent the Spirit from living through me?

The Sharing and Closing Prayer

If you liked *The Jesus Meditations*, don't miss these guided
meditation books from Fr. Michael Kennedy

Eyes on the Cross

"Can we muster the courage to walk with Jesus into that place of blood
and brokenness? East L.A. experiences that 'help us find God'"
--Martin Sheen
0-8245-1879-9 $14.95 paperback

Eyes on Jesus

"An extraordinary and insightful work for personal reflection on the
relevance of the gospels on our modern daily lives." --Martin Sheen
0-8245-1828-4 $14.95 paperback

Don't Miss these fine books from The Crossroad Publishing Company

Ronald Rolheiser
Against an Infinite Horizon

Do you ever feel that your meditation is just a small corner of the divine
in a difficult world? Bestselling author Rolheiser invites us to see
meditation, and every aspect of life, as part of a world filled with God
and brimming with possibility and hope.
0-8245-1965-5, $16.95 paperback

Thomas Keating, OCSO
Intimacy with God

This Trappist monk and former abbot teaches us the method of center-
ing prayer--a non-vocal prayer based on the desert fathers and mothers
and the work of St. John of the Cross.
0-8245-1588-9 $16.95 paperback

Robert Ellsberg
All Saints

A perfect birthday gift. These daily vignettes about saints from Teresa of
Avila to Gandhi and Martin Luther King, Jr. are "short, splendidly
wrought profiles. a richly imagined collection." -Kenneth L. Woodward,
Religion Editor, *Newsweek*
0-8245-1679-6 $24.95 paperback